AF433149

SONGBIRDS, SNAKES, & SACRIFICE

Other Works by Valerie Estelle Frankel

Henry Potty and the Pet Rock: A Harry Potter Parody
Henry Potty and the Deathly Paper Shortage: A Harry Potter Parody
Buffy and the Heroine's Journey
From Girl to Goddess: The Heroine's Journey in Myth and Legend
Katniss the Cattail: The Unauthorized Guide to Name and Symbols in The Hunger Games
The Many Faces of Katniss Everdeen: The Heroine of The Hunger Games
Harry Potter, Still Recruiting: A Look at Harry Potter Fandom
Teaching with Harry Potter
An Unexpected Parody: The Spoof of The Hobbit Movie
Teaching with Harry Potter
Myths and Motifs in The Mortal Instruments
Winning the Game of Thrones: The Host of Characters & their Agendas
The Girl's Guide to the Heroine's Journey
Choosing to be Insurgent or Allegiant: Symbols & Analysis of Divergent
Doctor Who and the Hero's Journey: The Doctor & Companions as Chosen Ones
Doctor Who: The What Where and How
Sherlock: Every Canon Reference You May Have Missed in BBC Series 1-3
Symbols in Game of Thrones
How Game of Thrones Will End
Joss Whedon's Names
Pop Culture in the Whedonverse
Women in Game of Thrones: Power, Conformity, and Resistance
History, Homages and the Highlands: An Outlander Guide
The Catch-Up Guide to Doctor Who
Remember All Their Faces: A Deeper Look at Character, Gender and the Prison World of Orange Is The New Black
Everything I Learned in Life I Know from Joss Whedon
Empowered: The Symbolism, Feminism, and Superheroism of Wonder Woman
The Avengers Face their Dark Sides: Mastering the Myth-Making behind the Marvel Superheroes
The Symbolism and Sources of Outlander
The Comics of Joss Whedon: Critical Essays
Mythology in Game of Thrones
We're Home: Fandom, Fun, & Hidden Homages in Star Wars the Force Awakens
A Rey of Hope: Feminism, Symbolism & Gems in Star Wars: The Force Awakens
Chosen One: The Heroine's Journey of Katniss, Elsa, Tris, Bella, and Rey
Hunting for Meaning in the Mandalorian

SONGBIRDS, SNAKES, & SACRIFICE

COLLINS' PREQUEL REFERENCES AND PHILOSOPHIES EXPLAINED

LitCrit Press
ISBN 979-8696249605

CONTENTS

INTRODUCTION

The Hunger Games delighted readers worldwide and created a new spin-off genre of dystopian fiction for teens – most centered on a sixteen-year-old rebel girl redefining her world. *The Atlantic* called *Hunger Games* heroine Katniss Everdeen, "the most important female character in recent pop culture history," and *TIME Magazine* named Katniss to its list of "The 100 Most influential People Who Never Lived." On The Hunger Games trilogy, *The New York Times Book Review* wrote, "At its best the trilogy channels the political passion of 1984, the memorable violence of *A Clockwork Orange,* the imaginative ambience of *The Chronicles of Narnia* and the detailed inventiveness of Harry Potter" ("News Room").

The Ballad of Songbirds and Snakes is set 64 years earlier, during Panem's Dark Days. Beginning on the morning of the repeating of the 10th hunger Games, the book tells the story of a teenage Snow, who finds himself mentoring one of the tributes of District 12. This book tells a new story—of a villain's descent into cruelty and of the philosophical device between permissive and tyrannical governments. "Suzanne Collins is a master at combining brilliant storytelling, superb world building, breathtaking suspense, and social commentary," said Ellie Berger, President, Scholastic Trade. "We are absolutely thrilled—as both readers and publishers— to introduce the devoted fans of the series and a new audience to an entirely new perspective on this modern classic" ("News Room").

Scholastic editor David Levithan notes, "We see the evolution of Snow and that's interesting. But to me, the more interesting part was seeing the evolution of Panem and seeing the Hunger Games in its tenth year and seeing how rudimentary it was and seeing how all of the themes and all of the ideas that we'll see later in the trilogy are having their origin story."

Published simultaneously in print, digital and audio formats by Scholastic in the US, Canada, the UK and Ireland, Australia, and New Zealand on May 19, 2020, while most of the world was on lockdown from Coronavirus, the book was a big hit. Many saw plenty of homages to the main trilogy as well as to the ancient philosophers. But who were these philosophers and what did they preach? The previous tributes and Capitol residents had carefully chosen names – do the new characters? And what are all the homages and nods, not only setting up the future but tying Katniss and Coriolanus together in their needs and desires? Let's read on…

Why Write This?

The Hunger Games arguably launched the era of fourth-wave feminism in which blockbuster action films could star a female protagonist. In her films, Katniss broke further ground by being fully, modestly dressed, for being deadly and competent, for sidelining her romance for heroism. The book pushed harder at barriers by suggesting Katniss with her "straight black hair" and "olive skin" might be multiracial, while her ally Rue is dark-skinned.

The prequel came out a decade later in the era of "We Need Diverse Books," as publishers and authors sought to bring minority heroes to center stage. Films had pushed forward too, finally creating the first superheroine films in decades, and arguably the most successful and iconic with *Wonder Woman* and *Captain Marvel,* among others. *Birds of Prey* and *Black Panther* joined the lineup to offer more diversity and less objectification.

After all this, many fans were surprised by the announcement that Collins' new book would follow Coriolanus Snow's formative years. Many posted something to the effect of "the one story we don't need is that of an oppressed, incredibly privileged white male." Others described the stories they'd hoped to hear – mostly about oppressed characters from District 12's past and future.

Nonetheless, the book went forward. Scholastic editor David Levithan explains:

> I think what's so exciting about the book is that it will appeal both to fans and to a new generation of readers. As to how we maintained this, we were lucky to have two editors on this project: my colleague Kate Egan and me. Kate reread the trilogy right before we started work, so it was fresh in her mind. I did not—so I represented all the readers who loved the books but who might not have stopped by Panem since the last book (or movie) was released. We had to make sure it worked for both of us—and it did. (Appell)

Levithan also notes, "I don't like him but I really am fascinated by him." As he adds, the villain's descent sucked him in: "As it became clear what Suzanne was doing with the character, both of us [co editor Kate Egan and himsefl] were totally enthralled."

As it turned out, the book offers two large tracks that make it better fit its era. Lucy Gray is an outsider even in District Twelve, as are her misfit family (one of whom was found by the roadside). As traveling entertainers from nowhere, they're symbolic minorities. While not an archer and warrior, she's clever, competent, and delightful with a confidence far beyond Katniss's. Like Katniss, she wins readers' hearts quickly with her dazzling performativity and understanding of the world. Collins throws in other diversity: A subtle male-male relationship and female-female relationship emphasize acceptance of homosexuality without dwelling on the relationships or presenting them as unusual. With so much hatred between oppressed and oppressors, no one cares to judge others for who they love.

The other surprise for readers is that this is decidedly not a story that evokes sympathy for Snow. He begins in a place of neutrality and suffering within his privilege, but this becomes the story of an increasingly unsympathetic villain's fall. As he learns from the vile Dr. Gaul, cultivates a philosophy of dictatorship, and betrays his closest companions with a sickly calculating expediency, all so he can "land on top," readers loathe him. Though he is the viewpoint character, Collins skillfully turns readers against him, teaching that using one's talents for cruelty is never the right choice. His privilege, his use of violence, his lack of love – all are held up for scrutiny.

It's a highly compelling story even with what should have been limited tension. Readers know that as he hopes in chapter one, Snow will someday become president and continue the games. The games themselves will gain more prominence and artistic cruelty with new luxuries for participants. Snow is destined to have a granddaughter, but likely not with a wild circus-dressed girl from the poorest district. Though he's banished from the Capitol, he'll find a way to return.

> We know, of course, going into this story, that Coriolanus, for all his charm, will become a monstrous tyrant; we know from the moment we meet her that sweet cousin Tigris will become maimed by body modification, trodden down by life, and so embittered toward her dear "Coryo" that she will aid his assassins; we know that Haymitch is the only District 12 Victor left alive by the time of the 74th Games. So we know, this will not be a happy story. Ballads rarely are. (Hardy, "Ballad")

Despite all this preparation for tragedy, or perhaps because of it, readers can't stop flipping as Coriolanus is treated unfairly (in his mind) and makes increasingly savage choices. It's the villain's journey, that of an ordinary teen into a treacherous supervillain, and it's oddly compelling. Many of these have been arriving too, with films and shows like *Maleficent, Joker, The Boys, Descendants, Megamind,* and *Despicable Me.* Other franchises like *Black Panther, Phantom of the Opera, X-Men, Star Wars,* and *She-Ra: Princesses of Power* are overshadowed by compelling, charismatic villains. All of these stress the new, more complex type of storytelling, with cardboard villains giving way to those with depth and purpose. This new book fits right in. Collins' editor David Levithan explains, "Rarely have I seen someone structure a

12

story as deliberately and as well as Suzanne. Editorially, I am by nature a tinkerer. But I know not to try to tinker with Suzanne's structure, because its calibrations are vital to the storytelling" (Appell).

SHAKESPEARE'S CORIOLANUS

Of course, Snow's first name is Coriolanus because that was established in the original trilogy. This, in turn, constantly references Shakespeare's *Julius Caesar,* with *nine* significantly named characters (Brutus, Cinna, Portia, Purnia, Flavius, Messala, Cato the Younger, Claudius, and Caesar himself) so that the trilogy appears a direct allegory about the power of propaganda and how the new dictator is no better than the one before. President Snow plays Caesar's part, but (likely because the name has positive correlations) he is instead named for Shakespeare's unsympathetic Roman who'd be happy to let the districts starve. Building on these allegories, this new book correlates well with Shakespeare's *Coriolanus* — better than the trilogy, in fact.

Shakespeare's *Coriolanus* takes place around 491 B.C.E., when Rome is in the early stages of a Republic run by elected officials. For the main plot, the celebrated warrior Coriolanus tries to win the Roman people's votes but fails and is banished to the provinces in disgrace. Building up his reputation there, he makes war against Rome. Beyond this larger story, smaller themes and connections link Shakespeare's play with Collins' novel. In Rome, men win honor and glory on the battlefield, in a society where mothers proudly raise their children to be soldiers. Likewise, teenage Snow considers heading "to officers' school, *elite* officers' school, where he could distinguish himself and find a way back to a life worth living." As he thinks, "This might even be a better road to power than the university had offered." The central theme in the play is the struggle between upper and lower classes and the question of what the ruler owes to his people.

The play begins with the plebeians, or common people,

desperate for food – as the patricians are accused of hoarding it all. In fact, the plebeians particularly blame Caius Marcius (later called Coriolanus) for his hard-heartedness, since he thinks only the military deserves the food. He's soon labeled "chief / enemy to the people" (1.1.7-8). Both cities struggle with wholeness thanks to damage of the class system. In Snow's world, the upper class have won but are still beset by hunger and misery so they turn to sadistic vengeance, torturing district children and then throwing them into the Hunger Games. Two of the tribunes of Rome, Brutus and Sicinius, privately denounce Marcius. Snow's world, too, is filled with backbiting.

A patrician named Menenius Agrippa tries to calm the rioters, providing a more public-sympathetic foil like Snow's friend Sejanus. Menenius' speech on the fable of the belly (I.1.91-150) describes the need for order: The citizens cannot operate without the senators any more than body parts can leave. Since the belly gets all the food in order to help the entire body, any revolution just shows ingratitude. In this speech, Menenius never actually addresses the peoples' biggest complaint, which is that they are literally starving. Instead, his friendly speech about how the senators should get everything wins them over by pandering to and manipulating them. In fact, the plebeians think Menenius is "honest" and call him "Worthy Menenius Agrippa, one that / hath always loved the people" (1.1.51-52).

In this way, he becomes a foil to Coriolanus, the play's least successful politician. Coriolanus always speaks his mind, succumbing to his emotions even when he tries to solicit votes and humble himself. Menenius functions as his spokesman and tries to do damage control but fails. As he tells the crowd later, Coriolanus is such a valiant soldier that he can't speak well in peacetime:

> Consider further,
> That when he speaks not like a citizen,
> You find him like a soldier. Do not take
> His rougher accents for malicious sounds,

> But, as I say, such as become a soldier,
> Rather than envy you. (3.3.70-75)

The plebeians call Coriolanus a lover of honor in I.i.30-40. Still, it's not clear whether this is enough to make him a good consul. As soldiers gossip about his bid for consulship, one officer replies, "That's a brave fellow; but he's vengeance proud, and loves not the common people." Next, they debate what they want in a leader: flattery, valiance, helpfulness.

After this, he leads the army to battle and wins. However, his innate Romanness puts him in opposition to his country. When the Roman army retreats from their enemy, the Volscians, he cries that they are "shames of Rome." As he calls them "souls of geese/that bear the shapes of men," he suggests that he's far superior (I.4.31-37). Further, if these are Romans, he rejects the cowardice they embody.

After he wins a great military victory, the people propose to make him Consul. However, to achieve this, he must dress humbly, go out on the streets, and solicit votes from the common people. This show of a humility he doesn't feel disgusts him, as he knows he's better than the plebeians. He tells the senators that their will should never take second place to the people's:

> If you are learn'd,
> Be not as common fools; if you are not,
> Let them have cushions by you. You are plebeians,
> If they be senators: and they are no less,
> When, both your voices blended, the great'st taste
> Most palates theirs. (III.1.1854-1859)

Likewise, when Snow sees the tributes emerge from the cattle car, "a wave of pity and revulsion swept through him. They really were creatures out of another world. A hopeless, brutish world." He brings Lucy Gray food, but his grandmother scolds him for eating with her and giving the impression of equality.

The play wonders whether all Romans are equal, or whether those of less prestigious insider birth than Coriolanus count. This of course reflects the Capitol-Districts conflict. At the play's beginning, Coriolanus sees himself as the ideal Roman and embodiment of their principles. "Unflinching courage, absolute devotion to the state, and by implication disdain for a 'Greek' predilection for reflection over action—these are the attributes that define the ideal Roman" (Hatlen 399). His tough and stately mother Volumnia has instilled them in her son. Moreover, Coriolanus embraces that identity. As he's been taught, "For human beings there is no 'self' outside of or prior to the political order" (Hatlen 397).

Snow as well has grown up as a paragon of Capitol families (or so he makes it appear to others). However, he hates the clumsy leadership that let him family starve and now bosses him around arbitrarily, with a weak, drug-addled hypocrite in charge of his school. He's struck by the injustice of torturing children for their parents' crimes (or rather, their parents losing a war). Coriolanus's disgust with the other senators echoes Snow's with the dean – both are certain they would rule better than those in charge.

The tribunes' desire to serve the people versus serve themselves becomes a major theme. Ambition is presented as leading to positive things but also evils of power and position. The politicians are not better people, though they are educated in philosophy and honor as well as strategy and war.

Stanley Cavell has proposed that the play "is not a play about politics, if this means about political authority and conflict, say about questions of legitimate succession or divided loyalties. It is about the formation of the political, the founding of the city, about what it is that makes a rational animal fit for conversation, for civility" (Hatlen 397). As another critic adds, the world working the way it should is central: *"Coriolanus* concerns itself largely with Order— Ordo—the harmony inherent in the State, the world, the universe when all things occupy their proper places and fulfill their assigned functions" (Neumeyer 192). The hero wants his civilization to carry on properly and feels tension when it doesn't.

In Act I, his name is formally changed to Coriolanus. The

18

name means he is "of Corioles," the city he has captured (I.10.65). He insists he became Coriolanus alone. "Alone I did it," he brags (V.6.122). When he defects to their side, the name takes on an alternate meaning, suggesting loyalty, not conquest. Later, returning to Rome, he refuses to answer to this or any other name. the name he presumably wants here is "Romanus," conqueror of Rome (Hatlen 416). However, he cannot become a true Roman by conquering his own city. By rejecting his people, he can never find acceptance.

> The play demonstrates the impossibility of identity in at least three ways. On the social level, Coriolanus attempts to define himself as an autonomous individual, only to discover that the self is always dependent upon the social ground on which it stands. Psychologically, Coriolanus struggles to separate himself from his mother, but finally fails. And on the linguistic level, he sets out to name himself, only to fail once again. On all three levels, furthermore, the concrete sign of Coriolanus's failure to become the "author of himself;" is a flood of shame, which thus serves to define the limit of personal identity, the moment when identity dissolves into contradiction. (Hatlen 394)

Young Coriolanus Snow has similar conflicts – following the rules puts him in conflict with his sense of honor and fair play. Maintaining a perfect exterior and hiding his disdain for everyone else also fails to save him. His name, his connections, his birth are all less secure than he had imagined. After his life lessons gained through exile and return, he constructs a new persona – the hated tyrant who will torture and kill children, but in so doing will stop the chaos he perceives around him.

Like Snow, Coriolanus considers himself superior to those from the districts. In Acts II and III, he struggles with the legal requirement that he present himself before the people and ask for their support before becoming consul – he is no longer a military leader, but a politician soliciting votes. Snow of course must court approval as well—in chapter one, he goes around offering empty compliments and properly self-deprecating humor. Later, Snow sings the anthem perfectly and thinks, "It was pathetic, but he needed every drop of approval he could get." When accused to his face of not loving the common people, the Roman Coriolanus responds by pledging to flatter them to be consul, though he's reluctant. He insists, with some amount of cringing at the hypocrisy of it all:

> I will, sir, flatter my
> sworn brother, the people, to earn a dearer
> estimation of them; 'tis a condition they account
> gentle: and since the wisdom of their choice is
> rather to have my hat than my heart, I will practise
> the insinuating nod and be off to them most
> counterfeitly; that is, sir, I will counterfeit the
> bewitchment of some popular man and give it
> bountiful to the desirers. Therefore, beseech you,
> I may be consul. (II.3.1528-1537)

Twice he tries to wear the required "gown of humility" but cannot stand it and berates the citizens he needs so much. Coriolanus attempts to curry favor and solicit votes as tradition demands. "That precisely is the one thing hardest for Coriolanus to do and well do the senators, who are ill-disposed to Coriolanus, know it. (Neumeyer 194). His problem is that faking a humility he doesn't feel revolts him because he knows himself to be better. He does wear the robe. However, "Chaos results because Caius Marcius Coriolanus is incapable of recognizing that the plebs, though they may at times act like beasts, are human beings; that he, though he is a great warrior, is a human being; and that the plebs as well as the patricians are part of the state" (Proser 509). Rumors of his arrogance spread, and the people turn against him. They have heard how he has mocked his show of humility, expressed loathing for them, and regretted giving them food instead of leaving them to starve.

It's Coriolanus's mother who counsels him to play the game and win the position he wants. She also confirms his lofty position while telling him to compromise, adding, "You are too absolute/Though therein you can never be too noble." "Volumnia, arguing that a judicious mixture of honor and policy is as effective in war as it is in peace, does not even suggest that such pragmatism is fully compatible with the hero's sense of honor, but treats it as an expedient lie" (Datta 99). Coriolanus is shocked when his mother and friends admit that he should lie to gain favor. "Acting a part is abhorrent to his nature. He defects to the enemy's camp not to wreck vengeance on the citizens and their leaders, who banished him, but to demonstrate to his friends, especially his mother, that they have acted as bad counselors all along" (Datta 99).

Snow too sees no purpose in pleasing people in the districts when, in his mind, the nobility of the Capitol should rule in all ways. Still, Snow's grandmother is perpetually aware of society's judgment and its perception. She must humble herself occasionally too, as when she offers tea to Mrs. Plinth, but she loathes doing so. Over and over, she tells her grandson to wear a tie to dinner, carry a clean handkerchief, maintain standards and establish that he's better than everyone else, though he should also be humble and friendly to social-climb.

Coriolanus repents and tells his mother he will do as she insists and win the title: "I'll return consul; / Or never trust to what my tongue can do / I' the way of flattery further" (III.2.2325-2327). He goes back to the senate and tries to pacify the people, but he fails. In Act three, Scene three, the tribunes banish Coriolanus from Rome and he refuses to beg people he considers inferior for another chance. He insists: "I would not buy/Their mercy at the price of one fair word" (III.3.2148-2149). Snow likewise accepts the dean's punishment of exile silently, knowing there's nothing he can say and not stooping to uselessly beg.

Coriolanus is nonetheless shocked that his friends, the senators, condemn him for pride and agree to his banishment instead of taking his side: "Coriolanus does not understand why the patricians, who have always supported his political philosophy and shared his contempt for the citizens, should fail to rally round him at the very moment when his derogatory views on the citizens are fully vindicated by the latter's revocation of the pledge" (Datta 99). When the sentence is carried out, he retorts:

> You common cry of curs! whose breath I hate
> As reek o' the rotten fens, whose loves I prize
> As the dead carcasses of unburied men
> That do corrupt my air, I banish you;
> And here remain with your uncertainty!
> Let every feeble rumour shake your hearts!
> Your enemies, with nodding of their plumes,
> Fan you into despair! Have the power still
> To banish your defenders; till at length
> Your ignorance, which finds not till it feels,
> Making not reservation of yourselves,
> Still your own foes, deliver you as most
> Abated captives to some nation
> That won you without blows! Despising,
> For you, the city, thus I turn my back:
> There is a world elsewhere. (III.3.2492-2507)

It is they, not he, who are banished, he insists. After symbolically banishing them, he appears to embody Rome all by himself, but in exile. He goes out to find the "world elsewhere" but it seems that there is nothing of significance outside his city. He goes to the enemy camp, insisting:

> My birth-place hate I, and my love's upon
> This enemy town. I'll enter: if he slay me,
> He does fair justice; if he give me way,
> I'll do his country service. (IV,4,2744-2748)

He joins his enemy the Volscians, but remains obsessed with his birth city. He is in limbo, "a kind of nothing, titleless/Till he had forged himself a name o' the fire/Of burning Rome" (V.1.13). With this, he returns to Rome threatening to conquer it – more as a hired gun than of his own volition.

When exiled himself, Snow is nearly suicidal with despair but still resolves to do his duty honorably, even while giving his heart to Lucy Gray and her District 12. He hides his identity, ashamed to admit who he once was and how far he has fallen. He also fears retribution from the people in the districts. His Roman namesake likewise hides his identity as long as he can. At last, he confesses his past, emphasizing the cruelty of Rome and their betrayal of him before he's resolved to do the same:

> The cruelty and envy of the people,
> Permitted by our dastard nobles, who
> Have all forsook me, hath devour'd the rest;
> And suffer'd me by the voice of slaves to be
> Whoop'd out of Rome. Now this extremity
> Hath brought me to thy hearth; not out of hope--
> Mistake me not--to save my life, for if
> I had fear'd death, of all the men i' the world
> I would have 'voided thee, but in mere spite,
> To be full quit of those my banishers,
> Stand I before thee here. (IV.5.2839-2849)

He vows his loyalty to the rebels, saying, "I will fight/Against my canker'd country with the spleen/Of all the under fiends" (IV.5.2856-2857).

At the climax, he prepares to invade and destroy his homeland. At this, his mother Volumnia, wife Virgilia, honorary sister Valeria, and little son Marcius all kneel before him to beg him to relent, and, thus confronted by his family, he yields. Arguably, it's the shame of realizing he cannot break his dependence on them to be perfect warrior and Roman. Why does he change his mind? Many reasons are presented. Volumnia stresses the dilemma of a son battling his own country and flatters his vanity before finally appealing to his duty to her. She warns that his name will be infamous. Further, her kneeling to him upsets the natural order – a circumstance that seems to repel him. He gives in, mostly from acceptance of the right path.

"When Coriolanus recognizes that he can never recover his Romanness by conquering Rome and accedes to his mother's pleas, his identity simply collapses" (Hatlen 403). He returns to the Volscians, even knowing they will discard him. It's a near-suicidal decision, so it's unsurprising he doesn't balk at death. "Coriolanus gives himself to the conspirators' swords as if he were already dead—as indeed he is, from the moment when, outside the gates of Rome, his struggle toward an identity collapses under its internal contradictions" (Hatlen

404).

Snow's fleeing into the wilderness is a similar type of suicide – giving up all his ambitions and future glory to fade from sight. However, his new path to officer school and his discovery of the evidence against him both offer a path for his triumphant return and eventual presidency.

Shakespeare's and Collins' Volumnia

Volumnia, Coriolanus's mother in the play, gives her name to Snow's mentor, Dr. Gaul. They share similar roles as the young leader's shaper, but also in their methods and morals. Both are overwhelmingly commanding personalities who control life and death. "Volumnia's name invites a psychoanalytic reading of this play, for she is voluminous, all-encompassing, engulfing. She claims to have made her son what he is, and he does not dispute this idea. Defiant toward all other influences, he cannot resist her wishes" (Hatlen 405). Coriolanus's mother, denied an active role in Roman society, lives through her son. He in turn flees to the all-male army to escape her.

Shakespeare's character is particularly heartless as a creator of character, whatever pain may result. She defines herself as the "perfect Roman mother" (ii.1.177-78). As such, she insists:

> Hear me profess
> sincerely: had I a dozen sons, each in my love
> alike and none less dear than thine and my good
> Marcius [Coriolanus], I had rather had eleven die nobly for their
> country than one voluptuously surfeit out of action. (I.3.384-387)

Volumnia persuades her son to stand for consul in Act 3 and not to conquer the city in Act 5. With such plot-shaping decisions, she directs the action – Coriolanus makes the choices, but she forces him to revise them when she disapproves.

> Coriolanus's pride may not derive entirely from her, but she is
> certainly involved in it. By encouraging him to be the surpassing
> warrior she desires, she helps to create that breach between him

> and the community which characterizes her. She may be able to
> see the political sense of "flattering" the plebs when her son's
> new consulship is at stake, but she dislikes people as much as he
> does, has always disliked them, and makes no bones about it.
> The result in Coriolanus is a kind of monstrous "honesty,"
> complex and self-defeating, which compels him to use his own-
> self image as a blindfold (Proser 507).

. As the puppet-master of his life, she's recreated well in Dr. Gaul. At the end, Snow's mentor reveals that all that's defined his life – the Hunger Games, his exile, his reinstatement – all have been directed by Gaul in order to teach him about the world. Shaped into a protégé who believes in her philosophies, he speedily ascends to gamemaker, determined to continue her legacy.

Other Characters

Cominius, a consul, sees Coriolanus as the perfect 'product' of Rome, explaining, "Rome must know/the value of her own" (I.9.20-21). He is loyal to Rome and leads the war effort. He also tries to maintain the status quo – so he fears riots as they threaten the social hierarchy. When the plebs get ready to fight at the marketplace, Cominius warns, "That is the way to lay the city flat; [...] In heaps and piles of ruin" (3.1.256, 259). He echoes the dean, desperate to prop up their government.

Tullus Aufidius, a powerful Volscian general and thus Coriolanus' arch-enemy, is not entirely like Sejanus, but not entirely different either. He's most notable for his obsession with Coriolanus: As it happens, he would "pawn his fortunes" to only be called Coriolanus's "vanquisher" (III.1.13-17). He resents his rival's fame and adoration by the common people. He initially appears a worthy opponent, but always loses. In Act four, scene five, their bromance seems positively erotic.

> Know thou first,
> I loved the maid I married; never man
> Sigh'd truer breath. But that I see thee here,

> Thou noble thing, more dances my rapt heart
> Than when I first my wedded mistress saw
> Bestride my threshold. (4.5.126-131)

After comparing Coriolanus to his bride, he goes into detail about the dreams he's had about encountering Coriolanus on the battlefield, insisting, "I have nightly since / Dreamt of encounters 'twixt thyself and me" (4.5.134-139). He pretends to be Coriolanus's ally in taking Rome, but tells the Volscian Senate of his partner's failings. He's willing to resort to trickery to win against the other man. When Coriolanus agrees to a peace treaty with Rome, Aufidius accuses Coriolanus of treason and finally kills him. One of the final images of the play is of Aufidius standing triumphantly on top of Coriolanus' corpse. So dies the tragic hero.

Tigris's parallel comes in Coriolanus's wife Virgilia. She is quite passive and silent, always deferring to her tougher husband and mother-in-law. When her husband is banished, she sadly barricades herself in her home and refuses to leave it. In all ways, she exists only as support to her husband. Still, she's observant and realistic: Only Virgilia sees her husband as human and fallible rather than a perfect warrior.

> By recognizing that Coriolnaus can die and that his death would be an irremediable loss to her, she affirms his connection to humanity and that human tenderness which he has almost buried from sight. And, significantly, it might be noted that Coriolanus consistently treats his wife with gentleness. Equally her affirmation suggests that across the gulf which might seem to separate two such different people as Coriolanus and Virgilia, there is a bridge, and that this bridge also connects Coriolanus with the plebs, whether he chooses to see it or not. (Proser 509)

Likewise, Tigris, who sympathizes with Lucy Gray, gives her cousin a bridge to humanity and the districts. Ultimately, however, both heroes do as they wish and are directed by the matriarch Volumnia more than by this younger woman.

SINGING AND PERFORMANCE

Even more than in the trilogy, songs here have deeper significant meanings. The first time Lucy Gray is seen singing is when she's chosen in the reaping. In place of the three-fingered signal, the crowd supports her another way. The people, presumably led by her covey, sing to her in support, and she sings with a chorus that insists no one can take anything from her she values. Presumably, she means the love of family, her pride, her showmanship, her spirit. After, back in District 12, she sings it again, and Coriolanus thinks, "the irony of [this] was not lost on the audience. The Capitol had tried to take everything from Lucy Gray, and it had utterly failed."

Of course, Lucy Gray and Katniss share a love of song. The former is a performer and latter considers singing private and deeply personal. Still, both can be seen inspiring the people with their tunes of revolution, especially shared ones. Her and Lucy's love of song can be seen as embracing subversion as well as art that's genuine in a world of lies.

> Katniss grows up in a world of lies – the Peacekeepers are really killers, the electrified fence is a sham. Her mother warns her to always act properly and obediently, teaching that appearance outweighs reality. Panem is a world of stories and storytellers: the Capitol maintains the fiction that they are in control, and Katniss and Peeta become storytellers powerful enough to take that control from them. Katniss strives to find truth, and as she does, she constructs a new tale. Connecting with her roots, she finds a power beneath that of Plutarch's staged propos – the influence of story and song. (Frankel, *Many Faces*)

Levithan points out that Lucy's motives are unclear throughout the story: "Because she is always a performer, you never really know where her thoughts lie or her affections lie or her strategy lies." Katniss, by contrast is very direct—and not just because she's the point of view character. As a performer, Lucy tends to be whatever the crowd wants and often holds back her rebellion to be deliberately likeable…again, unlike Katniss.

Katniss only reluctantly joins the world of showmanship, and in the third book, her friends decide that her best moments are the authentic ones in which she ignores the audience's demands. Lucy Gray, however, hurls herself into artifice. In the ballad of herself, she describes spreading kisses as part of her job – professionally charming others. While Katniss needs coaxing and commanding during her Capitol performances, Lucy Gray coaxes Coriolanus, teaching him how to shine.

She's a performer, in a brightly colored dress that makes Snow remember the circus. In fact, all this symbolism sets up that they're in the performance of their lives. Just as Katniss is always in the Games, whether being monitored at home or invading the Capitol, Snow is always in the spotlight, forced to offer an entertaining façade. In fact, he's thrown into the zoo truck and the monkey cage along with Lucy, for Capitol children to gape at. Lucy Gray reminds him to "own it" – to perform and show off, so he does. She also tells him the iconic mockingjay is part of the Capitol's show – the games – rather than her own small performances.

After, Coriolanus tells Dr. Gaul, "We fell in a cage and we landed onstage" (58). She approves, noting that he's learned to turn a witty phrase. Meanwhile, she's uttering rhymes comparing him to her lab rabbit. He and Lucy both are, but he hasn't yet learned to see it. With this, she suggests he be a gamemaker. Social climber that he is, he considers it a pointless job. However, he's missed her lesson that they're all in a manipulated world and being the manipulator, like herself, is thus the most powerful job of all. Snow takes his first steps as he presents Lucy as a star.

In the monkey cage, Lucy Gray sings "Down in the Valley" with new lyrics about taking a train and being in the Capitol jail. Those who sing the pretty song today may find this jarring. In fact, Collins has done her homework. The original lyrics begin with love as well as roses and a train call but soon grow darker:

> Ever a slave, dear
> Ever a slave
> Dying for freedom
> Ever a slave
>
> Write me a letter
> Sent it by mail
> And back it in care of
> The Birmingham jail

Guitarist Jimmie Tarlton claimed to have written the lyrics in 1925 while he was jailed in Birmingham, Alabama for moonshining. Folk musicians continued passing it along, making it something of a protest song.

When he hears "Down in the Valley," it reminds Coriolanus of his mother's loving lullabies. This opens a window to his past for viewers. At the same time, it suggests he's remembering his first warm emotions while he falls in love. As he starts caring for someone disadvantaged, he's opening his mind, not just to Lucy Gray but to a world of protests, complications, and rebellion.

> Of course, all the songs that Collins herself created for this novel or the original trilogy are literary ballads, as she wrote them, but, within the context of the books, particularly this one, they have specific roles. Songs like "Down in the Valley," which was likely composed in the early 20th century have, in the novel's distant future, morphed into folk ballads. Since I have spent the last ten years claiming that this was the "Valley Song" that Peeta tells Katniss he remembers her singing on the first day of school, winning his heart, I feel very vindicated in my claim after *The Ballad of Songbirds and Snakes*. We also see the composition of literary ballads that function as broadsides, as Lucy Gray crafts her own story in "The Ballad of Lucy Gray," and as she is revealed to be the creator of the haunting "Hanging Tree." (Hardy, "Ballad")

Hardy adds that this book, pointedly titled *The Ballad of Songbirds and Snakes,* indeed is filled with ballad motifs. It offers star-crossed love, a mystery ending, rose imagery, whiteness and snow, burning hot weather, furious storms, treachery, hidden murders and secret crimes, and dramatic tragedy. "Three people are hanged in *The Ballad of Songbirds and Snakes*, because three is the magic number" (Hardy, "Ballad"). Like "The Hanging Tree" these events have become semi-recalled history, muddled and retold until one assumes no one will remember the exact truth of Lucy Gray's winning the games and falling for the future President Snow. His secrecy on it and the records being buried adds to the mystique. The novel's mirroring the climax of Wordsworth's "Lucy Gray" also calls its ballad motifs into prominence.

Performing for the crowd in her interview before the games, she sings "The Ballad of Lucy Baird Gray" to win herself sponsors. It's "haunting" while her voice is husky from the smoke and sadness. She sings of a couple – he stole and gambled while she danced and kissed, but he grew angry about her past and left her. Soon she'll be dead, and he'll be alone. Still she knows all his secrets. This is an actual story of her past, meant as a code for her Covey to settle the score. At the same time, this feels like a warning to Coriolanus – if he betrays her, she knows many of his secrets. Further, this truly serves as an introduction, with her life story blending with a depiction about the toughness of life in District 12. Fulfilling the song's other goal, she receives sponsors and acclaim. Like the tributes in the trilogy, she's introducing herself through a performance, but this is more literal. The audience love her because she looks like "someone who still knew how to have fun" (169). This is something they've lost in the war and postwar time – there are no entertainers anymore.

When Coriolanus enters the arena to tour it, the automated voice chirps ludicrously "Enjoy the show," though performances have been replaced a decade prior with a brutal slaughter (135). Of course, the tour turns into a slaughter of its own when bombs suddenly go off. With this, Coriolanus must realize that he's part of the show – as much of a pawn as Lucy Gray. When he is forced into the arena to rescue Sejanus, the automated voice chirps "Enjoy the show" a second time. Here, he's being recorded, watched, and judged by gamemakers, as he tries to rescue Sejanus who, using his insight as a philosopher, realizes he's no better than the arena children. Snow must face this same realization even as he too must perform as the gamemakers demand. As he thinks in horror, "He was just like the subject of [Dr. Gaul's] other experiments, students or tributes, or no more consequence than the Avoxes in the cages" (229).

Back in the safety of the gamemakers' room but still recorded by reporters, Coriolanus asks Dr. Gaul to take a bow after her snakes are unleashed and kill several tributes. As the camera switches from the games to them, he's clearly aware of his required performance. Later, Sejanus criticizes the essay Dr. Gaul makes them write on why they all loved the war adding, "As if it had been some big show" (343). Coriolanus, too, recalls the pageantry and excitement, like a sports game everyone was watching together. He brings the same camaraderie to the games by trying to get viewers more involved. With betting and sponsors, as the dean describes it, "It means we're all in the Arena together" (274).

The true showman here is Lucy Gray, who sings to entrance the snakes and ends with a multicolored skirt of them. This epic image not only stuns Coriolanus, but viewers everywhere. Her sponsors pour in offerings. Moreover, she wins the games by trickery, encouraging the other tributes to do what she desires then subtly poisoning them. Even more than her likability, her beguilement helps her succeed.

When Coriolanus finds her in District Twelve, she sings a love song that pleases the crowd. Once again, there are deeper themes. Onstage, Lucy sings about how her heart will keep "a-crawlin' back to you." While it's a popular entertainment song, it suggests the connection between her and Coriolanus, a relationship that keeps parting and reuniting them.

Maude Ivory follows with "My Darling Clementine," which Coriolanus regards as a funny song about a girl's death. So it is. It's a popular western song from the mid-1800s, possibly based on a Mexican ballad brought north by Gold

Rush miners. It integrated well into pop culture, making it a logical choice for her to sing with the audience. Of course, the theme of death as ludicrous and commonplace in a brutal, uncaring world matches Snow's view of the districts.

For a special salute, Maude Ivory takes the stage later and sings "Lucy Gray," the Wordsworth ballad. The setting is changed slightly, with the wild moor and minister clock updated to a vague village. Otherwise, Maude's version is the same as the original with the child getting lost and mysteriously dying. Of course, the ending is ambiguous. Maude Ivory speculates that the heroine didn't die but instead changed into a bird. As she adds, "I think she flies around and tries not to meet people, because they'd kill her because she's different" (432). Clerk Carmine adds that she's haunting the place. Lucy Gray's imagery as bird and ghost is repeated through the book, while this ending foreshadows her own.

Coriolanus dislikes this wild, haunting song. In fact, listening to the folk songs, he thinks, "Some of the numbers bordered on unintelligible, with unfamiliar words that Coriolanus struggled to get the gist of, and he remembered Lucy Gray saying that they were from another time" (364). When they Covey sing along in complex harmonies, "Coriolanus didn't care for it; the sound unsettled him. He sat through at least three songs of this kind before he realized it reminded him of the mockingjays" (365). When he's asked to sing, the national anthem is the only song Coriolanus knows. His and his grandmother's repeated singing of the one formulaic, compulsory tune contrasts with Lucy Gray's creative performativity. All of their music contrasts with the Capitol anthem as wild and emotional, and it repels him.

The Covey are named for particular ballads, as described in the names section.

> ...the metaphorical birds are the real stars of the show. Lucy Gray is a singer, musician, and songwriter who creates and performs songs Hunger Games readers have heard before, as well as actual traditional songs and originals. She lives with her stage family, called the "Covey," a word that is generally applied to groups of birds, like quail, but which also has slang uses from the

> 18th and 19th centuries, primarily when used by the lower classes or criminal elements of society. "Covey" or "'Cove" can be used like "fellow" or "dude" (It is the term with which the Artful Dodger first addresses Oliver Twist), but, according to the *1811 Dictionary of the Vulgar Tongue,* a "covey" can also refer to "a collection of whores." All of these meanings are wrapped up in Lucy Gray's band/family, who dress in bright colors that often include feathers, and who all sing and play, like songbirds. In addition, they represent a lower echelon of society, regarded as lower-class, even in District 12, and the possibility that Lucy Gray might sell more than her songs is one that rankles at a jealous Coriolanus. (Hardy, "Ballad")

A Covey refers to a flock of birds, and Lucy Gray calls them her pretty birds. Coriolanus thinks, "Birds. Always birds with her, when it came to the Covey. Singing, perching, feathers in their hats. Pretty birds all" (421). When Coriolanus worries the Covey are trespassing in their usual backstage shed, deliberately evoking her covey's bird imagery of freedom, Lucy replies, "We'll just perch here until they shoo us off" (421). Dr. Kay tells him that some people just understand birds, and "Coriolanus felt unequivocally that he would never be one of those people" (413).

His first encounter with "The Hanging Tree," the meadow lullaby, and other songs of District Twelve take on new meaning as one assumes Katniss's performances must prove a particular sticking point in his old age.

> Although he is charmed by songbird Lucy Gray at the novel's outset, Snow's discovery, late in the novel, that perhaps he doesn't actually like music at all, is a brilliant twist that lines up neatly with the uses of music in the original trilogy and makes us wonder now, more than ever, what odd thoughts might be going on in Snow's bitter mind as he plays his mind games with Katniss, a girl whose Cinna-designed clothes echo the lurid colors of the Covey, who may even be a descendant of one of the band members, whose singing must put him in mind of Lucy Gray (especially when she sings to dying Rue), and whose emblem, the Mockingjay, is the songbird he most loathes even before it spells doom for his empire. (Hardy, "Ballad")

Katniss's future existence helps foreshadow the tragedy as readers know all these songs will be repeated when a girl from

12 defies Snow as tyrant.

By the lake, Lucy sings Maude the meadow song. It's a loving lullaby as it is in Katniss's life (leading many to suspect Maude is Katniss's paternal grandmother). Katniss calls it "a simple lullaby, one we sing fretful, hungry babies to sleep with. It's old, very old I think. Made up long ago in our hills. What my music teacher calls a mountain air." As such it matches the Covey's other songs. While most are depressing, about betrayed love and loss, with the lullaby, as Katniss thinks, "The words are easy and soothing, promising tomorrow will be more hopeful than this awful piece of time we call today." Nature itself is cast as protective, as the daisies guard the listener. Having Lucy sing this by the meadow adds to the sweet and peaceful imagery. In *Catching Fire*, it's Katniss's image of the utopia she craves: "As I drift off, I try to imagine that world, somewhere in the future, with no Games, no Capitol. A place like the meadow in the song I sang to Rue as she died. Where Peeta's child could be safe" (pp.364-5).

> Rue's death and Katniss' bedecking her corpse with flowers are scenes that echo throughout the rest of *Hunger Games* and *Catching Fire* — think of the District 11 salute she receives on the Victory tour, Peeta's confronting the Games Makers with Rue's icon, and its prequel echo in Haymitch's farewell to Maysilee Donner in his Quell — but this song, a lullaby that infants trust as truth, is, because of its age and meaning, the primordial aspect of life transcending Panem that Katniss taps into as her core strength and surety. As we've just read above, she returns to this forgotten meadow paradise in her Quell on the beach when she commits herself to serving Peeta even at the cost of her life. (Granger, "Katniss's Meadow Song")

Entertaining the crowd again, Lucy sings another song about betrayal with a chorus of "I'll sell you for a song." This has a creepy parallel with Coriolanus's betrayal of Sejanus, committed through the jabberjays. Certainly, she's singing about Billy and foreshadowing Coriolanus and herself, but the layers resonate darkly. Moments later, Coriolanus bursts in on Sejanus's deal and two people are killed. The song makes it clear that no one can be trusted as the pleasant status quo is shattered. During the killings, Maude Ivory is onstage singing "Keep on the sunny side of life," an ironic juxtaposition as violence tears them apart. Her perpetual optimism cannot save them.

At the Commander's birthday, Lucy Gray sings again. There is a deeper message for Coriolanus though he fails to hear it: Her song hints at her relationship with Billy and how trust is all that matters to her. She chooses the one "pure as driven snow" (481). Also, as she starts the song by noting that everyone's born innocent, she stresses her own philosophy. Still, as she blames her unfaithful lover with "you tell me lies, I can't stay true" in another song, Snow's betrayal, current and future, is alluded to as well (456).

Musicals repeat songs, often with a twist, to evoke the earlier mood or flip it. Lucy Gray's singing "Down in the Valley" and the reaping song in her scene entertaining District 12 does this, as do repeats of "The Hanging Tree." As Maude Ivory reprises "Keep on the Sunny Side," Coriolanus finds himself imagining a life with Lucy Gray. For a few moments, borne on the current of the song, he actually lets himself be optimistic. However, Lucy closes off with a more ominous song as she sings the complete "The Hanging Tree" and urges Coriolanus to meet her there. The image of the pair with ropes around their necks finishes off the invitation. The book's final song is a reprise of 'The Hanging Tree" when Coriolanus is chasing her through the forest, and she sings as diversion. The mockingjays imitate it, creating a surreal world in which forest, music, water, and "The Hanging Tree" all battle him until he gives up and flees. Coriolanus believes she's singing the song to reveal she knows of his betrayal of Sejanus, but he's exceptionally paranoid at this point. She may be singing of their hopeless situation or even calling on one of them to run, but he fails to understand.

Katniss realizes the hanged man calls to his lover because "the man wants his lover dead rather than have her face the evil that awaits her in the world" (*Mockingjay* 291). Parting from Peeta and Gale in the war, Katniss imagines them captured and thinks of "The Hanging Tree." "Combined, the two songs become a question posed to Peeta and Katniss: will fear, torture, hate, lust for power, and the desire for self-preservation ultimately prove to be so strong that even lovers would betray each other?" (Borsellino). Katniss and Peeta's love survives the test. Katniss understands that the goal is not just remaining alive but keeping one's humanity. Coriolanus, however, gives this up in his book's climax. His and Lucy's story becomes that of "The Hanging Tree" as much as "Lucy Gray." Lucy's song about the hangings indeed follows the ballad tradition:

> The Broadside Ballad is based on real events, re-told in the sensational format of a catchy tune. Very often, these events involve a murder, so often that broadsides are sometimes also called murder ballads. More often that not, the murder is of a young woman; "Little Omie Wise," "The Banks of the Ohio," and "Tom Dooley," all follow that theme, although the actual, historical events are greatly altered by artistic license. Broadside composers frequently took just enough of an actual story to get credibility, and then created a completely fictional narrative. Such is the case of "The Ballad of Frankie Silver," which is written as if from the point of view of Frances (Frankie) Stewart Silver just before she was hanged, right up the road from me, in 1833 for killing her husband with an ax (and cutting up the body, which was not found all at once. Charlie Silver famously has three graves). Frankie Silver wrote no such thing. The best-researched account of the story is *The Ballad of Frankie Silver*, by the incomparable Sharyn McCrumb, who gives the doomed Frankie, whose crime was almost certainly committed to save herself and her child from a drunken abuser, one of my favorite lines in all literature: "Happy stories mostly ain't true." (Hardy, "Ballad")

When reading the original trilogy, many compared the forbidden song "The Hanging Tree" to "Strange Fruit," a song that protested lynching in America. There's also the connection to the dystopian world of *1984*. Winston thinks of an old song lyric: "Under the spreading chestnut tree/I sold you and you sold me." In the decades between books, the song seems to have taken on extra meaning, to the point that Katniss doesn't know the story of the original. John Granger explains:

> I suggest "The Hanging Tree" of *Mockingjay* was also a "movement" song or anthem and that the meaning of the lyrics were not as important as what it may have come to mean to the rebel miners in terms of what caused the Capitol to make it illegal.
>
> In essence, "The Hanging Tree" calls on the living who love freedom to join the martyred freedom fighter in putting this cause above concerns for their individual lives. It is an invitation to revolution, i.e., to risk death in the hope of a greater life. Mr. Everdeen isn't singing it because it's a simple catchy tune; he's expressing his revolutionary beliefs as openly as he dares and asking others to join him. Mrs. Everdeen, it turns out, was right to be terrified by her husband's boldness. It's probably safe to assume that he and Gale's dad died in a mine explosion that was set by the Capitol to kill men known to be plotting against the regime. (Granger, "The Hanging Tree")

The new volume reveals the story that inspires "The Hanging Tree" and thus adds to its meaning. Its story echoes the song: Lucy indeed chooses death or fleeing into the wilderness over perpetual slavery. Snow, however, embraces the system, deciding to perpetuate it and someday rule it. He fails to learn the song's lessons. Snow, who appears to have never truly loved, tries using love against Katniss in the trilogy. This backfires, however. "By making Katniss emphasize her love story in *Catching Fire*, Snow does more to incite the rebellion against his Capitol than Katniss could have achieved on her own" (Rees).

> A few hundred years ago, if you did something wrong you were physically punished—beaten or even hanged, usually in front of a crowd. The whole point of this was to warn the people watching—if you do something bad, this could happen to you.
> Except it didn't quite work. Because if you're watching a starving thirteen-year-old girl being flogged for stealing a loaf of bread, you're not thinking about what a terrible person she is, and how you'd better not ever do anything like that. You're thinking, That poor girl. She only wanted something to eat. And the people who are doing the punishing don't want you to feel sorry for her. (Wilkinson)

Snow learns this lesson in scenes like Sejanus's hanging, where the crowd sympathizes with how childlike he and Lil appear. He likewise watches Lucy Gray's attempt to win over Capitol citizens and make them care for her. Still, he fumbles it in *Catching Fire* as he makes Katniss submit to the reaping in her wedding gown, and she and Peeta get the audience out of their seats screaming for their adored young couple (now allegedly married and pregnant) to be freed.

Snakes establishes that Lucy wrote the song and that her Covey, especially Maude, will continue singing it, even if she is dead or vanished. Is Katniss's father, who sings and knows this subversive song, descended from the Covey? Or just taught in their tradition? Collins adds:

> Focusing on the 10th Hunger Games also gave me the opportunity to tell Lucy Gray's story. In the first chapter of *The Hunger Games*, I make reference to a fourth District 12 victor. Katniss doesn't seem to know anything about the person worth mentioning. While her story isn't well-known, Lucy Gray lives on in a significant way through her music, helping to bring down Snow in the trilogy. Imagine his reaction when Katniss starts singing "Deep in the Meadow" to Rue in the arena. Beyond that, Lucy Gray's legacy is that she introduced entertainment to the Hunger Games. ("Scholastic Releases")

Songbirds

Embracing her songbird status, Lucy Gray sings frequently throughout the novel, even using her lyrics to convey covert messages. Katniss as mockingjay shares this image, tying Lucy Gray into her future rebellion. Both teens love mockingjays and sing with them. The birds themselves are images of wild nature surviving despotism. "They hadn't anticipated its will to live," Katniss concludes (*Catching Fire* 92). Mockingjays aren't fighters, but hidden survivors, much like Katniss and Lucy, who sneak into the forest and try to hide from Peacekeepers. Katniss comments, "I am the mockingjay. The one that survived despite the Capitol's plans. The symbol of the rebellion" (CF 247).

Both girl and bird are kind of hybrid. Katniss's mother comes from the upper class and her father from the Seam. She is a child and a breadwinner, a pawn and a revolutionary, a young girl and a warrior. Further, the mockingjay isn't a construct but a natural product of its environment. Like Katniss, it wins admirers with sweet songs and independence, not by doing what the Capitol intends.

Birds are creatures of heaven and spirituality, like angels. Mockingbirds are so-named because they playfully imitate other birdcalls. Of course, a mockingbird in particular evokes *To Kill a Mockingbird:* in this book, the bird represents the innocents who do nothing but make the world sweeter but are sacrificed without reason. This is a strong theme in *The Hunger Games* as well. (Frankel, *Many Faces*)

Coriolanus's views of jabberjays and mockingjays reflects his philosophy. He finds the birds repellent and off-putting — "nature run amok." He considers music an "invasion" in his life that distracts him and keeps him off balance like Lucy herself (445). It's also notable that he likes cats, the domesticated and thoroughly tamed predators that devour birds: Pluribus's white cat is named "Boa Bell," a nightclub-related name that nonetheless offers a snakelike image. She's white — a color evoking his own preferences.

He loathes nature and freedom, which reflect humanity's natural state. Like Dr. Gaul, he wants everyone controlled, much as he sees the helpful, obedient jabberjays once the Capitol has remade them to its liking. These birds are like the apocryphal "canary in the coalmine" — a foreshadowing of how he will betray Lucy Gray in her wildness and ally himself with the more diabolical Dr Gaul and her terrible mutts.

The mockingbird, prolific and common, with its whimsical gift for imitation, is the ideal counterpoint to the (seemingly) sterile and artificial jabberjay created in a lab for the sole purpose of spying on the Capitol's enemies. The mockingjay, then, brings together the opposing elements of freedom and control, nature and science, and makes the ideal symbol for the rebellion against the Capitol's stifling control over its far-flung empire of districts. (Hardy, "Bird's Eye")

As Coriolanus chases Lucy through the woods in the climax, mockingjays echo her song and rise in dizzying clusters, like the forest itself rising to protect her. They sing "The Hanging Tree," and Snow decides they're all blaming him for betraying his friend to death. In this scene, nature itself rebels at who he has become.

Both animals of the title not only feature in the plot but work as metaphors for it – the jabberjays symbolize spycraft and treachery as a means to control the people of the districts. Mockingjays, as Katniss and Coriolanus both observe, are wild, chaotic, rebellious nature that embarrasses the Capitol through its very survival. And snakes not only suggest treachery but "are an omnipresent reminder that a life can end in just one strike" (Hardy, *Ballad*).

Snakes

Just as Katniss is the "girl on fire," Lucy Gray quickly becomes "the girl with the snakes." Her first act in the book is to drop a live snake down the dress of her rival, the Mayor's daughter. This imagery is interesting not only because the heroine is associated with a traditionally treacherous and creepy symbol. It also belongs to Snow in the other books: When Katniss first encounters Snow up close at the end of *The Hunger Games,* Katniss specifically describes his eyes as being "as unforgiving as a snake's." Likewise, in the first chapter of *Catching Fire*, Katniss is startled by the appearance of Snow and his "snakelike eyes" in her house. Katniss isn't surprised Snow is a poisoner, as she thinks it's "the perfect weapon for a snake" (*Mockingjay* 172). His "pale, sickly green" skin also emphasizes the connection as he sits dying in his rose garden (*Mockingjay* 355). The title *The Ballad of Songbirds and Snakes* slightly suggests that one character will embody one, and one, the other, especially since they are opposites. (Further, it employs *Hunger Games* imagery in which Katniss is the mockingjay bird and Snow, as shown here, is the treacherous snake.) Instead, this becomes the story of Snow's encounter with the snake-

and-songbirds girl and his own fall into treachery.

Lucy Gray tells him, "I saved you from the fire and you saved me from the snakes. We're responsible for each other's lives now." She says this is "written in the stars" which evokes Peeta and Katniss's fake "star-crossed lovers" routine as well as the actual Romeo and Juliet who fail to escape society's condemnation of their relationship (386).

When Lucy survives the snake attack in the games, crooning to them and cradling in her rainbow skirt until they merge with it, creating "a brilliant skirt of weaving reptiles," she is a mystic, goddesslike figure (301). Still, something seems untrustworthy about this moment, as if she has an unearthly power (or is cheating in the games, or both). Even Snow is mesmerized. Having her use a snake as a murder weapon afterwards is surprising but fits the story well – she lacks the great stature and fearsome weaponry of her attacker, and instead sics the snake on him, killing him quickly in a moment that resembles an embrace. It's a moment of duplicity but also seduction of a sort. Coriolanus parts from the Capitol impressed and obsessed with her, yet a little wary.

It should be noted that matriarchal cultures saw snakes as positive, an image of wisdom and feminine regeneration. In fact, in the rose garden, Snow's truth-telling is reminiscent of the snake in the Garden of Eden, who tells Katniss how to find wisdom. As Merlin Stone notes in her groundbreaking *When God Was a Woman,* "Despite the insistent, perhaps hopeful, assumption that the serpent must have been regarded as a phallic symbol, it appears to have been primarily revered as a female in the Near and Middle East and generally linked to wisdom and prophetic counsel" (Stone 199). Snakes coiled around many Great Goddess statues such as Asherah, Ishtar, Athena, and Hathor. They represented the goddess's cycling, as she went from young to old, pregnant to shrunken.

The other snake character is the goddesslike matriarch Dr. Gaul who cultivates rainbow-colored snake mutts and other prototypes that let her maim and torture animals as well as her own students. Gaul's creatures kill and mutilate her chosen victims – basically everyone they encounter except Snow and Lucy. Both have literal protection by having their scents absorbed, but they also have symbolic protection as the snakes do not turn on anyone as duplicitous and flexible as themselves. She's a paragon of knowledge used for evil purposes, a bit like the snake in the Garden. The mutts, as Katniss notes in the final book, are meant to damage people with "a perverse psychological twist": the tracker jackers bring insanity, the jabberjays, terror for one's family (311):

> No mutt is good. All are meant to damage you. Some take your life, like the monkeys. Others your reason, like the tracker jackers. However, the true atrocities, the most frightening, incorporate a perverse psychological twist designed to terrify the victim. The sight of the wolf mutts with the dead tributes' eyes. The sound of the jabberjays replicating Prim's tortured screams. The smell of Snow's roses mixed with the victims' blood. Carried across the sewer. Cutting through even this foulness. Making my heart run wild, my skin turn to ice, my lungs unable to suck air. It's as if Snow's breathing right in my face, telling me it's time to die. (*Mockingjay* 311)

Katniss describes facing lizard creatures that are self-destructive in their vicious rage: "Lashing out with tails and claws, taking huge chunks of one another or their own bodies with wide, lathered mouths, driven mad by their need to destroy me" (*Mockingjay* 311). With this, *Mockingjay* stresses that all these new weapons are fundamentally evil. These also cause Snow's slow downfall – he drinks from a cup of a poison he has concocted and is poisoned enough to constantly bleed from the mouth, with "mouth sores that will never heal" a condition that appears inevitably fatal (*Catching Fire* 172).

Of course, Lucy's snakes are natural, like the forests, mockingjays, and food plants that surround her. She describes the snake she put on the mayor's daughter as a beloved pet. By the lake, Lucy knows where the snakes lurk. She also stresses that their duplicitous nature, like her own, makes them appealing. She adds that trust is more important than love and adds, "I mean, I love all kinds of things I don't trust. Thunderstorms…white liquor…snakes. Sometimes I think I love them because I can't trust them, and how mixed up is that" (441).

Accordingly, Coriolanus's stress dreams in District Twelve feature the colorful snakes, which represent danger and death one cannot escape or outwit. In one, the dream switches between the snakes and his kissing Lucy Gray, suggesting she represents a similar unpredictable danger for him.

In the climax, the snake that apparently tries to kill Snow is harmless and has no fangs – like Lucy herself. Notably, it is the snakebite, after, in his mind, he is lured close with Lucy's scarf, that makes him believe she is trying to kill him. He shoots wildly in response, and she vanishes. His own paranoia has separated them forever. "What President Snow never understands it that choosing love over survival is the ultimate act of defiance Katniss can make. It's not one or the other: the love and rebellion are one and the same." (Borsellino). While Lucy retreats into the forest, joining with her natural world forever, Snow turns to ice.

Snow's Symbols

Snow's imagery already cast him as the destroyer the plant children: Katniss, Rue, Primrose, the Hawthornes, and all the others. "Actual snow is of course frigid and can kill, in the same way katniss can nourish. Snow is the enemy of food plants, flowers, harvests, and growth, though it does far less to inconvenience those living in cities" (Frankel, *Katniss*). In this novel, the name suggests his coldness as he learns to wall himself off from love. In fact, in the final pages he decides to marry someone he'll never love as a way of keeping aloof and controlled.

The boiling hot summer of the novel suggests a crucible where everyone is cooked down to their essence, much like the games. Twice, Snow brings Lucy ice as a gift. This provides a respite from the suffering of District 12 and symbolizes Lucy Gray and Coriolanus getting a brief breeze of happiness together. It represents himself, with no riches or luxuries to offer anymore save for what the Capitol allots him. Notably, the ice is artificial, dispensed from a machine and placed in a plastic bag. It's thus incongruous and foreign to District Twelve, a sign of the mass production Snow admires.

While his name is central, reinforced in this novel with jokes like "Snow lands on top," roses appear nearly as often, in another deliberate homage. In this book, they also resonate because of their frequent presence in romantic ballads of star-crossed lovers, which this one turns out to be:

> Snow's roses are not just his symbol; they appear in countless ballads, enforcing those themes of love and death. Two of my favorite uses are in two of my favorite ballads: the aforementioned "Barbry Allen" (a rose grows from the grave of broken-hearted Sweet William and twines with the briar that grew from the grave of his cold-hearted lover Barbara) and "Tam Lin" (breaking a magical rose summons the lost-lost Tam Lin, who has been spirited off by the Fey). (Hardy, "Ballad")

However, their status as a romantic symbol is twisted, just as it is in the original trilogy (as the president showers the ground outside District 13 with them and Katniss is creeped out). Coriolanus and Lucy wear matching pink roses "in case anyone needed a reminder of who Lucy Gray belonged to." Over and over, his feelings are expressed as possessive and then prideful before loving. Likewise, his first gift to her of a white rose is meant to win her over, a gesture of perceived rather than true respect. Collins explains, "For whatever reason, Snow has a very controlling personality. Then he experiences one of the most out-of-control emotions, falling in love. It turns out to be a bad combination" ("Scholastic Releases").

His roses, as artificially formed as the ice cubes, get a backstory here, as his grandmother prides herself on cultivating them. They're a sign of affluence and luxury, available year-round as they are. She gives them to Coriolanus and Lucy as status symbols to show off their beauty and perfection. Looking at the one Coriolanus wears, the dean mourns that the games are evil, "After all the agonized promises to remember the cost. After all of that, I can't distinguish the bud from the blossom" (131). This imagery could be comparing the inspiration for the games (the original war) to the current unending violence. More subtly, it also compares Coriolanus to his father. The teen thinks they are nothing alike, but the dean sees the same betrayal and cruelty present in both.

At this point, the roses don't mask the smell of blood, but they show off Capitol citizens' control over nature as they grow the flowers in a controlled environment, out of season and strangely colored. They emphasize Grandma'am's wealth and artificiality, as they're available year round to those she snobbishly favors.

> Contrasting with the humble dandelion are hothouse roses, the most pampered and popular of luxury flowers. If Katniss, the simple hunter-gatherer, is a cattail root, Snow will always be the larger-than-life flowers that fail to provide nourishment but can fill an entire room with their overpowering, commanding scent. Worse yet, the rose's heady perfume covers the scents of blood and effects of poison that have become Snow's signature weapons... for Katniss, these hothouse roses are another of the Capitol's mutts, separated from nature and bred to please the jaded citizens. In the final book, Katniss enters Snow's magnificent greenhouse where he forces the roses to bloom out of season in the exotic, unnatural colors of the Capitol itself. They are "lush pink, sunset orange, and even pale blue" (*M* 354). Gardens like Snow's greenhouse have always been considered a symbol of man's power over nature, a palace for royalty and the rich (Chevalier and Gheerbrant 419). Though the garden is beautiful, it echoes the dungeons or the Games where Snow imprisons so many District children with their flower names. (Frankel, *Katniss*)

Through the novel, Coriolanus clutches his mother's rose-scented powder in her lovely, silver, rose-engraved compact. It's leftover from a time of luxury, and the dean describes Mrs. Snow's fragility and flightiness, like this delicate, frivolous item. Besides a symbol of love and comfort, the compact becomes a knightly favor for Snow's lady Lucy. This is reversed from the traditional heraldic pattern, as he gives it to her and she goes into battle, flipping the gender roles while he waits behind. This casts her as the more active character while he is more passive. She clutches it when thinking of him, hard enough to leave an imprint in her palm. However, as with many lover's tokens in many ballads, its discovery proves Coriolanus's treachery towards his home, and he is banished.

> The compact's cover is in the shape of a silver rose. Not only does this image create a cold, sterile rose image that lines up well with the Snow we'll know in the future, but the image previews one that may have seemed unimportant when we first read *Mockingjay:* the inlaid silver flowers in the cheeks of Plutarch Heavensbee's assistant Fulvia Cardew. That detail might have been completely meaningless without one of the last thoughts we overhear from young Coriolanus in *The Ballad of Songbirds and Snakes.* As he ponders the fact that he doesn't like being in love and will choose, if he marries, a woman he actually hates so that he won't be hurt by her, he lights on one of his classmates and fellow mentors, a girl he dislikes very much, Livia Cardew. We have to wonder then, if Plutarch's assistant, who defects with him to 13, is, like Tigris, a Snow family member who has grown to despise him. (Hardy, "Top Ten.")

Young Coriolanus adds to his keepsakes a stack of family photos and his father's compass. In fact, the image of his father provides a great deal of direction for Coriolanus, who imagines the stoic, honorable soldier living and dying for duty. Ironically, the one time Coriolanus uses the compass, it's to navigate into the wilderness with Lucy – the opposite choice of his father and the one place Coriolanus does not wish to go. He soon changes his mind. Lost in the storm of the climax, he finds the compass remains undamaged and helps guide him – like the memory of Capitol loyalty and devotion to duty and the military, for which his father died. As the novel puts it, "Coriolanus clung to the compass, a lifeline in the storm…feeling his father's presence beside him. Crassus might not have thought much of him, but he'd wanted his legacy to live on and perhaps Coriolanus had somewhat redeemed himself today?" (505).

At the end, his mother's makeup has melted away as have the family photos. His maternal loving influences are gone and his tougher father, symbolized by his compass, survives, pointing the way to cruelty. He regains the compact, but it's been emptied, used to poison others and finally lies empty and soulless, much like himself. This emphasizes how much he's destroyed his softer side. In fact, he buries it so deeply that lacks all understanding of it by Katniss's time, leading to his downfall.

COLLINS' BIG METAPHOR STARTS IN THE EPIGRAPH: HOBBES, LOCKE, AND ROUSSEAU

Suzanne Collins explains:

> Here's how it works now. I have two worlds, the Underland (the world of *The Underland Chronicles* series) and Panem (the world of *The Hunger Games*). I use both of them to explore elements of just war theory. When I find a related topic that I want to examine, then I look for the place it best fits. The state of nature debate of the Enlightenment period naturally lent itself to a story centered on Coriolanus Snow. ("Scholastic Releases")

This becomes clear from before the story begins: The epigraph in the preface offers quotes from Hobbes, Locke, Rousseau, and Mary Shelley's *Frankenstein* as well as a Wordsworth poem. The quotes explore how men turn evil and also the central philosophies of how the world works. The book's editor, David Levithan, adds, "She approached it really because she wanted to talk about the philosophy behind it and human nature and sort of…the Locke versus Rousseau battle turn into sort of who Snow becomes. And that was fascinating to me."

Hobbes

The quote from Hobbes' *Leviathan* explains: "Hereby it is manifest that during the time men live without a common power to keep them all in awe, they are in that condition which is called war; and such a war as is of every man against every man."

Thomas Hobbes (1588–1679) and John Locke (1632–

1704) had opposing views about the ability of people to govern themselves. Hobbes, shaped by the English Civil War, believed that the natural state of mankind (the "state of nature") is a state of war of one man against another, with man selfish and brutish. In fact, Hobbes believed that people in an original state of nature are primarily interested in preserving their own lives, even if that means killing or other immoral acts. Everyone's self-interest creates conflict as people fight over resources. To avoid perpetual war, people must agree to a social contract not to harm one another. However, because people are so cruel and selfish, they must be forced to obey. Hobbes thus decided that the ideal government is an absolute monarchy with maximum authority, subverting mankind's natural savage state and creating societal order in the process.

Sentence one of *Songbirds and Snakes* reveals that young Coriolanus lives in the most exclusive penthouse but survives on cabbage soup. He grew up during a savage war like Hobbes and writhes at the injustice of his suffering, mostly at the hands of the masses. Levithan points out that many fans expected a hero turning bad, but Snow is flawed and selfish from the beginning, making a more complex journey. "His personality was what it was but it was outside forces that either amplify pieces of who you are or help you go a different direction, and you see those, that tug of war, in this book." Snow has also grown up with his grandmother's emphasizing that he's a Snow, better than the outsiders she calls savages. In chapter two, he meets them at last.

Crammed into the circus cage with the district children, he's disgusted by their unwashed smell. As he decides, being cooped up with them lowers him to the level of the dregs he believes they inhabit. Further, he sees them as a mindless threat, as "feral animals devouring a pampered poodle" (45). The story even somewhat supports this as Lucy keeps them from attacking by pointing out that the Capitol may hurt their families before adding that she needs him. This scene depicts the children as dangerous and violent, needing a threat of reprisals to keep them from immoral acts. Granted, these children have been treated savagely and unfairly condemned to death, but as Snow sees them, they support his outlook. The Hunger Games only confirm his impression:

> Coriolanus thought about what it had felt like to be in the arena, where there were no rules, no laws, no consequences to one's actions. The needle of his moral compass had swung madly without direction. Fueled by the terror of becoming prey, how quickly he himself had become a predator, with no reservations about smashing Bobbin to death. He'd transformed, all right, but not into anything he was proud of – and being a Snow, he had more self-control than most. He tried to imagine what it would be like if the whole world played by those same rules. No consequences. People taking what they wanted, when they wanted, and killing over it if it came to that. Survival driving everything. (291)

He decides that people need to agree to follow laws in a "social contract," with law behind it. This is the essence of Hobbes' philosophy – that the world will resemble the Hunger Games if laws aren't made and enforced. Having had this epiphany, as Dr. Gaul had been guiding him, Coriolanus writes the theory up for her. As he concludes, "Without the control to enforce the contract, chaos reigned. The power that controlled needed to be greater than the people – otherwise, they would challenge it. The only entity capable of this was the Capitol" (292).

To Coriolanus, war isn't a romantic adventure but part of survival. "What he desired had little to do with nobility and everything to do with being in control. Not that he didn't have a strong moral code; certainly he did. But almost everything in war, between its declaration and the victory parades, seemed a waste of resources" (182). He grimly chooses to enforce his morality on others, to use torture and cruelty to prevent total destruction. As Snow tells the dean, there's a particular reason to put children in the Games. "Because we credit them with innocence. And if even the most innocent among us turn to killers in the Hunger Games, what does that say? That our most essential nature is violent"

(515).

Coriolanus describes Dr. Gaul's goal of keeping the games going "to punish the districts and remind us what beasts we are" (343). He describes her animal torture as an essential part of her philosophy: "I think that's how she thinks we all are. Natural-born killers. Inherently violent...The Hunger Games are a reminder of what monsters we are and how we need the Capitol to keep us from chaos" (343). On his adventures, he's won over to her philosophy. As he finally explains to her, "They're not just to punish the districts, they're part of the eternal war. Each one is its own battle. One we can hold in the palm of our hand, instead of waging a real war that could get out of our control" (508-509). Hobbes likewise believed man's normal state was that of perpetual war, and thus people needed controlling with their violent urges properly directed. Dr. Gaul reframes the Hobbsian beliefs as chaos, control, and the contract and urges Snow to write about them and investigate them.

The difficulty is that the leader enforcing the laws can be seen as cruel...and often is. Dr. Gaul coldbloodedly lets her snakes bite her student Clemensia because she thinks lies conceal weakness. She's a tyrant who does whatever she wishes, thanks to her power over the students. She uses her terrible mutt hybrids to torture others for her amusement, as Coriolanus thinks in horror. However, it turns out that her cruelty has its own authoritarian morality – she tortures Clemensia, but only after the girl lies. She banishes Coriolanus to the districts so he can learn. Even the monsters she breeds are tools to promote fear and obedience.

Clemensia is an interesting case – in the games, she refuses to feed her tribute because she's trying to change his behavior. In this way, she acts as the authority. However, he is engaging in moral behavior – refusing to kill and shrouding the dead tributes – though Clemensia thinks he's disrespecting the Capitol by ignoring his duty in the games and ripping down the flag. As all her fellows clamor at her to feed him, she models despotism.

The mutts continue to play a role is the war between tyranny and freedom. On arriving at District 12, Coriolanus is creeped out by the forest and the mockingjays. Over and over, he views them as nature "running amok" and needing to be tamed. He soon accepts the jabberjays, which are controllable with the press of a button. There are particularly suggestive moments, when he tries to shoot the mockingjays and catch them in baited traps but the birds evade him both times. This works as a metaphor for several things that revolt him – Katniss in the future, but also District twelve's and Lucy Gray's freedom as he wants them both managed by a wise authority like himself. To him, mockingjays are the rabble. If he can't control them like jabberjays, he wants them dead.

Hobbes' view of life as nasty, brutish and short, particularly for the underclass, grows vivid here. Newly arrived in District 12, Coriolanus thinks of it with symbolism like that Hobbes himself might use: "His life, tragic and pointless, unspooled before him. He saw himself in twenty years' time, grown stout and stupid, the breeding beaten out of him, his mind atrophied to the point where nothing but base, animal thoughts of hunger and sleep ever crossed it" (337). Sejanus sympathizes with the starving people in District 12, but Coriolanus insists, "They lost the war. A war they started. They took that risk. This is the price they pay" (398).

Basically, Rousseau believed people were naturally good (an idea explored in *Frankenstein*) and Hobbes believed they were naturally bad. In District 12, Snow and Lucy Gray debate philosophy – he takes the Hobbesian approach that people are monsters and will kill each other without a strong government restricting their rights. Lucy meanwhile cherishes freedom as Coriolanus does control: He likes knowing the jabberjays have been returned to their lab, while Lucy says, "I hate to think of them caged up, when they've had a taste of freedom." Still, Coriolanus insists, "I know the Capitol must seem hard-line out here, but we're just trying to keep things under control. Otherwise, there'd be chaos and people running around killing each other, like in the arena" (434). She retorts that her family has given up too much for this, as they can't travel, sing the songs they want, or even stay together. "What if I think that price is too high to pay? Maybe my freedom's worth the risk" (435). Later, as they run away together, Coriolanus calls people "mostly awful" while Lucy Gray replies, "People aren't so bad, really…It's what the world does to them. Like us, in the arena. We did things in there we'd never have considered if they'd just left us alone" (492). In her view, people are good unless monstrous circumstances warp them.

On returning to the world of *The Hunger Games*, Suzanne Collins said, "With this book, I wanted to explore the state of nature, who we are, and what we perceive is required for our survival. The reconstruction period ten years after the war, commonly referred to as the Dark Days—as the country of Panem struggles back to its feet—provides fertile ground for characters to grapple with these questions and thereby define their views of humanity" ("News Room"). Her use of the phrase "state of nature" as well as the epigraphs shows how much this was the idea she wanted to explore—humanity's essential nature. (In fact, *Lord of the Flies,* to which this series is often compared, takes a Hobbesian view as well.) Scholastic editor David Levithan explains of *Songbirds and Snakes,* "the book engages larger philosophical issues about power and personhood. It's striking that they are as relevant now as they were a decade ago…or hundreds of years ago" (Appell).

The games function as a crucible that boils everyone down and reveals their true nature. In the larger series, Peeta fears he'll become a monster, and he does indeed prove himself to the Careers and join them, though he also sacrifices himself for Katniss. Tough Katniss turns kinder, sparing the others what pain she can. In just a few minutes in the games, Coriolanus beats a child to death with a plank. "Coriolanus thought about what it had felt like to be in the arena, where there were no rules, no laws, no consequences to one's actions. The needle of his moral compass had swung madly without direction. Fueled by the terror of becoming prey, how quickly he himself had become a predator." On the first day of this game, the first kill is Lamina's mercy-kill of Marcus. Just after, Reaper comforts Dill, who's dying of tuberculosis. Clearly, some of the tributes still feel empathy. However, before the readers can hope that these children are all inherently kind, Treech steals Dill's water, leaving the other child to die. Increasingly violent deaths follow, and even Lucy kills to save herself and win.

Of course, in such an oppressive world, surviving the hunger games doesn't bring safety or success. There is a much larger game going outside the arena, and everyone is a pawn, save for the few gamemakers manipulating the players. At last, Dr. Gaul "wins" the novel by accomplishing her goal – turning Snow into the perfect Hobbesian protégé and future dictator. In both their views, this will preserve their society. As he thinks, "He'd continue the Games, of course, when he ruled Panem. People would call him a tyrant, ironfisted and cruel. But at least he would ensure survival for survival's sake, giving them a chance to evolve" (516).

However, as Collins suggests throughout the series, the savagery of the Hunger Games is a bad response, victimizing all levels of society. She sees them as a tool of tyranny, adding, "In the book, the annual Hunger Games themselves are a power tool used as a reminder of who is in charge and what will happen to citizens who don't capitulate," Collins notes (Blasingame 726). This message is, none-too-surprisingly, contained in Shakespeare's play:

> What Coriolanus and the community fail to recognize is that the "heroic" image...contains a threat to themselves as well as to their enemies. They do not see how the cultivations of violence even in an outwardly acceptable military guise in a sense prepares the soul for any violence; nor do they seem aware that violence, though restricted to the formal patterns of war, is still at its heart irrational and may turn, in its being cultivated, with

> more ease than might have been anticipated against those who
> enshrine it in any form. (Proser 508)

The book ends with Coriolanus determined to become President Snow, the cruel leader who makes the Hunger Games into a larger, crueler spectacle in order to control its citizenry and maintain the Capitol's control…even though this cultivates the violence that will topple him decades later.

Levithan points out that at the time of the tenth games, the games could have been made less punative or even canceled, but the characters go darker instead. "I think there are lessons to be learned about human nature and about human societies and governments that we would really do well to listen to." Collins adds, "But given all that, you still need to leave room for Snow's personality. Is he a product of nature or nurture? Everyone of his generation experienced trauma, loss, and deprivation. And yet Sejanus, Tigris, Lucy Gray, and Lysistrata turned out very differently" ("Scholastic Releases").

Locke

The kinder characters of the book oppose Snow's philosophy, echoing other revered philosophers. For John Locke, the bloodless overthrow of King James II in the Glorious Revolution of 1688 (in which the people decided they wanted a different monarch and simply exiled him) showed how governments and civilized people should behave. According to Locke, the natural condition of mankind is characterized by human freedom and equality. As his epigraph reads, "The state of nature has a law of nature to govern it, which obliges every one: and reason, which is that law, teaches all mankind, who will but consult it, that being all equal and independent, no one ought to harm another in his life, health, liberty, or possessions…" As it concludes in *Two Treatises of Government,* "When his own preservation comes not in competition, ought he, as much as he can, to preserve the rest of mankind, and may not, unless it be to do justice on an offender, take away, or impair the life, or what tends to the preservation of the life, the liberty, health, limb, or goods of another."

Locke believed humans belonged to God and owed him moral behavior including remaining alive and preserving his gifts. Murder and suicide are thus proscribed. Further one's liberty, health, and property are necessary to preserve oneself. These are natural rights, and all people have them equally. Because they are so fundamental, no one should endanger any of these. Locke added that natural law, in which people behave naturally, is insufficient to keep all people protected, so laws are necessary to protect people's lives and property. As Locke goes on, people voluntarily create a "social contract" in which they give the government some power in order to protect their "natural rights" of life, liberty, and property. If the government does not fulfil this task, it's people's natural right to create a better government. Because of all this, the public has the right to resist authority—this is inherent and unable to be compromised. Thomas Jefferson, of course, adapted these ideas into the Declaration of Independence.

Sejanus Plinth, the rebellious student from District 2, may or may not have read Locke, but he understands his beliefs. He insists to Dr. Gaul, "You've no right to starve people, to punish them for no reason. No right to take away their life and freedom. Those are things everyone is born with, and they're not yours for the taking. Winning a war doesn't give you that right. Having more weapons doesn't give you that right. Being from the Capitol doesn't give you that right. Nothing does" (160). This reference to inalienable rights to live safely is directly Locke's philosophy. After this, Sejanus's speech is punctuated by his trying to leave and discovering he's locked in Gaul's classroom as definitively as the tributes are locked in the monkey house – all are pawns with the mentors no better than the tributes. Though Sejanus is privileged, he discerns that they all lack freedom and human rights.

Sejanus, the figure of morality in the story, brings the tributes food because he recognizes that they're children like himself and don't deserve to starve. Further, he encourages his peers, like Coriolanus, to help him. Throughout the games, he believes faithfully in others' goodness. He protests, "Who wants to watch a group of children kill each other? Only a vicious, twisted person. Human beings may not be perfect, but we're better than that" (81). Sadly, events of the series prove him wrong – as the games become more of a spectacle, watchers find them increasingly compelling.

Sejanus also puts his life on the line to protest injustice in a way few characters in the series do. "Have they all joined hands? Taken a vow of nonviolence?" Finnick asks Katniss sarcastically (*Catching Fire* 276). The children of the tenth game mostly don't (although Reaper stages his own protest, refusing to kill and instead respectfully laying out the dead, as Katniss does with Rue and Lucy Gray does with him). Sejanus, however, enters the games determined to martyr himself. He tells Coriolanus, "It's the only way I might possibly make a statement. Let the world see me die in protest" (234). Coriolanus only convinces him to leave by insisting that his protest won't be shown, so he should fight to change things in person. Sejanus accepts, adding that it's his responsibility to "end this whole atrocity somehow" (235). Peeta and Katniss also subscribe to some aspects of this philosophy, as both resist being turned into murderers within the games. Katniss similarly saves Peeta from suicide and self-sacrifice, insisting he must survive to fix the system beside her. Katniss, Peeta, and Sejanus fight the system, but finally discover that humanity's will for destruction is too strong. Collins adds:

> Well, I thought about Wordsworth's line, "The Child is father of the Man." The groundwork for the aging President Snow of the trilogy was laid in childhood. Then there's Locke, who's all over this book, with his theory of tabula rasa, or blank slate, in which we're all products of our experiences. Snow's authoritarian convictions grew out of the experiences of his childhood, as did his complicated relationships with mockingjays, food, the Hunger

> Games, District 12, District 13, and women. So, you rewind and
> plant the seeds. ("Scholastic Releases")

While Hobbes considered humanity's natural state equivalent to a state of war, Locke saw them as opposites: Humans are ordinarily kind and respectful and must violate this natural state to kill others. In fact, the state of war only comes about when someone proposes to violate someone else's rights. Thus, in Locke's theory of war, there will always be an innocent victim on one side and an unjust aggressor on the other. Certainly, the games and the brutality toward the districts follows this logic – either the Capitol or the districts must suffer under oppression, and Dr. Gaul and Snow both choose the districts to be the losers.

To Locke, slavery is the state of being in the absolute or arbitrary power of another. He defines slavery as a moral way to punish an unjust aggressor defeated in war. Tyranny in other circumstances, however, is forbidden. Coriolanus continues to adapt some of this logic. By the 74th Hunger Games, his propaganda film stresses that the districts are the aggressors here, and therefore their punishment is just (though as Katniss and Sejanus note, the children were born later and are not responsible). President Snow, aware of people's inherent understanding of justice, frames the games as well as the districts' starvation and totalitarian levels of discipline as consequences the districts have brought on themselves.

Locke also developed the innovative idea that people had complete rights over their own bodies—an issue of freedom and dignity due to all. The Capitol defies this through not only the deadly games but through smaller, crueler acts like thoroughly searching Lucy Gray to find everything hidden in her massive skirts and starving the children while putting them in the monkey cage to be gawked at. In Katniss's time, she's stripped and subjected to awful beauty treatments while treated as an object. Clearly, in the intervening years, the Capitol has gotten less respectful of people though in a more cruelly refined system.

Rousseau and Frankenstein

Rousseau's preface quote comes from *The Social Contract*: "Man is born free; and everywhere he is in chains." Jean-Jacques Rousseau (1712-1778) believed that people are born good but poverty, violence, and other threats of an unjust society turn them into monsters. In his writing, he suggests a new kind of government, in which each person will enjoy the protection of the common force whilst remaining as free as they were in the state of nature. The system will be based on the collective will of the citizens, who form a government to suit their goals. In obeying the law, each citizen is thus subject to his or her own will, and consequently, according to Rousseau, remains free. The Covey model this peaceful, utopian self-rule. If Lucy Gray were to build a government, she would choose this kind. Lucy tells Coriolanus, "The Covey believe you're put on earth to reduce the misery, not add to it" (434). In fact, the paradise of her past and future is of wandering through the wilderness in a tiny democracy, unconstrained by city rules but living as her family chooses. When Billy Taupe betrays her, he is banished from the Covey, who continue living as they will.

Of course, Lucy Gray feels her people shouldn't be trapped in District 12 or hurled into the brutality of the Hunger Games. Rousseau agrees, as he's particularly against tyranny and writes in *The Social Contract* that to renounce freedom in favor of another person's authority is to "deprive one's actions of all morality" as the renunciation of freedom is contrary to human nature. While Coriolanus thinks people need controlling, Lucy Gray believes people are decent and can police themselves, explaining, "I think there's a natural goodness built into human beings. You know when you've stepped across the line into evil, and it's your life's challenge to try and stay on the right side of that line" (493). When she sings in District 12, she asks the people to contribute voluntarily, if they can afford it. She trusts them, and through this trust, makes enough to live on. Much of her living is thus made by offering her gifts for free in a model that appears to work.

The *Frankenstein* epigraph at the beginning supports this mindset: "I thought of the promise of virtues which he had displayed on the opening of his existence and the subsequent blight of all kindly feeling by the loathing and scorn which his protectors had manifested towards him." This is not a horror novel, but a gothic unfolding that also puts Rousseau's theories into practice. It offers a constructed being created as a blank slate with unlimited potential. The creature is completely benevolent. Only constant cruelty and mistreatment, as the quote emphasizes, turn him violent. Certainly, the entire *Hunger Games* series stresses this, with characters from Peeta to Cato explaining that the games have made them killers.

Lucy Gray saves Coriolanus twice – once in the circus truck and once in the bombing. By doing so, she embodies the concept that people are fundamentally decent and will do the right thing. Coriolanus, who is more suspicious and self-centered, wonders why she helped him instead of running away during the bombing. She continues to role model for him, risking her life to sit with Jessop as she dies. As Coriolanus notes, this is in her character.

The non-philosophical epigraph is a Wordsworth stanza from his poem "The Tables Turned." Collins offers the second to last stanza of this longer work:

> Up! up! my Friend, and quit your books;
> Or surely you'll grow double:
> Up! up! my Friend, and clear your looks;
> Why all this toil and trouble?
>
> The sun above the mountain's head,
> A freshening lustre mellow
> Through all the long green fields has spread,
> His first sweet evening yellow.

Books! 'tis a dull and endless strife:
Come, hear the woodland linnet,
How sweet his music! on my life,
There's more of wisdom in it.

And hark! how blithe the throstle sings!
He, too, is no mean preacher:
Come forth into the light of things,
Let Nature be your teacher.

She has a world of ready wealth,
Our minds and hearts to bless—
Spontaneous wisdom breathed by health,
Truth breathed by cheerfulness.

One impulse from a vernal wood
May teach you more of man,
Of moral evil and of good,
Than all the sages can.

Sweet is the lore which Nature brings;
Our meddling intellect
Mis-shapes the beauteous forms of things:—
We murder to dissect.

Enough of Science and of Art;
Close up those barren leaves;
Come forth, and bring with you a heart
That watches and receives.

The poem contrasts the beauty and freedom of nature with book learning – a metaphor for Lucy Gray's and Coriolanus's worldviews, as each has embraced one of these lifestyles wholeheartedly. For instance, Coriolanus enjoys test-taking. "He loved the challenge and his obsessive nature meant almost instant absorption into the mental obstacle course" (405). Feminizing nature just strengthens the imagery. In their final adventure, Lucy Gray has invited him, as Wordsworth puts it, "Let Nature be your teacher," but Coriolanus quickly decides he's not suited for the lifestyle. Further, the sixth stanza's suggestion that one can learn better morality from nature than from sages offers Coriolanus an alternate path – Lucy's path – but he refuses to take it. Stanza seven, the one Collins quotes, is interesting since it directly seems to allude to jabberjays, mutant snakes, and other horrific mutts from Dr. Gaul's lab. It emphasizes how much humans with their learning pervert and destroy nature – a theme Katniss repeatedly learns as she contrasts her beloved forests with the Capitol's inventions. She is the humble, life-sustaining katniss plant and the mockingjay that thwarted the Capitol with its will to survive. Since she sings in the meadow and finally brings her children there, she can be seen as fully opening her heart to nature. Snow, however, fails to bring an open heart, and rejects all nature offers. The mockingjays in their wild rebellion and the earthiness of the forest repel him. Once he returns to the city, he continues instead to cultivate roses in the greenhouse that's like a prison where he can control nature.

> ...these hothouse roses are another of the Capitol's mutts, separated from nature and bred to please the jaded citizens. In the final book, Katniss enters Snow's magnificent greenhouse where he forces the roses to bloom out of season in the exotic, unnatural colors of the Capitol itself. They are "lush pink, sunset orange, and even pale blue" (*M* 354). Gardens like Snow's greenhouse have always been considered a symbol of man's power over nature, a palace for royalty and the rich. (Frankel, *Katniss*)

While introduced to other philosophies and arguing them with Lucy Gray and Sejanus, Coriolanus puts his own more brutal philosophy into practice by betraying them both and questing to make the games more brutal, even as he controls everything around him, from his future marriage to the roses that mask the smell of blood.

Some speculate that Lucy Gray found her way not to Canada but to District 13 and became either President Snow's great nemesis cold, gray-eyed Alma Coin or Alma Coin's mother. This seems a stretch, mostly because Coin fails to understand love. She coerces Katniss to vote for a final Hunger Games with district children and her blindness to Katniss's real loyalties leads to her death. Lucy Gray would have to transform not only to someone who's forgotten all love to someone who never understood why a District Twelve girl would fight to keep someone like Maude Ivory safe and further, executes the hopeful District Twelve medic Prim. It's out of character. Still, it would be intriguing if Lucy, who understands so well the art of performativity to make herself likable passes the traits on to her daughter Alma – to use all her powers of persuasion to incite loathing and contempt. If Lucy's daughter grew up hearing how District Twelve was better than Thirteen, with love, music, and fellowship, if she spent her life listening to her mother mourn the Covey and Maude Ivory – then, perhaps, she might turn on Katniss's family. It would of course be truly tragic if she became Snow's mirror through this warped upbringing. Both reveal themselves as willing to sacrifice anyone to maintain their own power and the structure of society – the ends justify the means. "Coin not only plans to have Katniss conveniently killed, a move worthy of Snow, but her plans after the rebels take the Capitol and imprison Snow show that her own innate corruption and evil matches Snow to the letter" (Rees).

KIDS IN CAGES: COLLINS TACKLES AMERICA'S ISSUES

In chapter one, Collins lists many things people in our country take for granted: Food other than cabbage soup and mushed potatoes. Buying new clothes instead of remaking them. Ration coupons. Coriolanus even considers the luxuries of garbage pickup – not only having the Avoxes to collect it but being able to throw out suspicious food and unwanted materials instead of frantically scrounging them for burning or insulation. All this is a product of the postwar culture. As Coriolanus grew up, bombs fell constantly, frightening everyone with the constant specter of death. During the war, the city was embargoed for two years. Now, goods are returning, but many remain poor. There's wreckage everywhere. In fact, the elevator is broken so the grandma rarely can even leave. Symbolically, their wealth has trapped them.

This image of shortages and isolation may resonate particularly with readers as the book came out during the height of the coronavirus pandemic. It accompanied massive, almost unprecedented job loss, with many struggling to feed their families. With so many staying at home, systems like electricity felt less dependable, adding to the stress and uncertainty. Most of all, there was the frantic hoarding of food and cleaning products. Coriolanus's life mirrors this – though it's illegal, his family piles up thirty crates of lima beans that must be kept a secret. When their cook leaves, they're forced to learn to boil them into unpalatable meals that nonetheless keep them alive. Coronavirus has resulted in more cooking at home, more hoarding of dried beans and canned goods, and of course, more relying on these staples.

With meat-packing planets in distress, America may be eating more beans yet.

Of course, the family's isolation for a different cause resonates even more. Young Coriolanus cannot have friends over and his cousin's attempt at romance falls apart because she's keeping her boyfriend out of the house. Grandma'am, particularly fragile, must be protected from everything. She, in particular, cannot leave the house. Her clothes are "so outdated as to be laughable now," as Coriolanus thinks. Certainly, at the time of publication, many were losing track of the outside world and shuffling around in house slippers as she does.

However, all this is somewhat coincidental as the book was written before the virus. Indeed, Collins appears to be protesting a recent cause more fitting with the book's timing.

While Katniss and Peeta get the royal treatment with the finest food they've ever eaten and a luxury apartment, the children in the tenth games are treated much more brutally. The kids are put on livestock cars, their hands bound, and beaten when they leave them. As innocents tortured for their birth, this echoes with the Holocaust and other moment of historical brutality, made worse by the victims' youth. Then the tributes are put in circus cage trucks and thrown into the monkey pen in the former zoo. There, as Coriolanus thinks, "Capitol children gawked at him." They're even treated by a veterinarian.

The obvious parallel is the caged migrant children at the border. During the Trump administration, the public became increasingly concerned of the plight of asylum seekers. Those who entered legally, fleeing persecution in destabilized countries, had their children locked up separately, for an indefinite amount of time, often with no documentation to assure their return. The Flores settlement, an agreement in the California case *Flores v. Reno,* set national standards for the detention, release and treatment of all undocumented children in federal custody. It requires the government to house the children it does detain in facilities that are "safe and sanitary" and provide "access to toilets and sinks, drinking water and food as appropriate, medical assistance if the minor is in need of emergency services, [and] adequate temperature control and ventilation." US law prohibits holding children in Border Patrol custody for more than 72 hours in typical circumstances. However, new policies ignored these laws.

In April of 2018, Former Attorney General Jeff Sessions announced the Trump Administration's Zero-Tolerance Policy for unauthorized immigrants -- to deter migrants the government would separate immigrant children from their parents so that the parents could remain in immigration jail for prolonged periods. After more than 2,300 children were taken from their parents at the border, President Trump issued an executive order to end family separation but then attempted to rewrite policy to allow for immigration officials to jail children indefinitely. "The Trump administration's proposed termination of the Flores Settlement agreement isn't just odious because it could detain families indefinitely. As in, years. It's also odious because it is an attempt to inflict cruelty on immigrant children and use them as pawns in a battle against adults," an editorial writes ("A New Cruelty").

The goal of torturing the children as a deterrent to adults links this present-day story with the tributes' plight. Why are guards torturing and mistreating them? Because of the circumstances they were born into, not for anything these children did. Likewise, as Sejanus observes, the tributes were ages two through eight during the war. None attacked the Capitol or perpetrated atrocities. All are completely innocent of the war, as they are in Katniss's time.

The acting Deputy Washington Director and Senior Researcher on Immigration in the US Program at Human Rights Watch, Clara Long, interviewed children and reported that "the US Border Patrol is holding many children, including some who are much too young to take care of themselves, in jail-like border facilities for weeks at a time without contact with family members, or regular access to showers, clean clothes, toothbrushes, or proper beds. Many were sick. Many, including children as young as 2 or 3, were separated from adult caretakers without any provisions for their care besides that provided by unrelated older children also being held in detention." The children interviewed had been wearing the same clothes for weeks. They were not given regular access to soap, toothbrushes or showers. When Covid-19 struck, guards spread it around, while forbidding children to wear masks. Children are not allowed to call their frantic parents even once to say where they are. Clara Long concludes, "Based on our interviews, US officials at the border seem to be making no discernable effort to release children to caregivers while children are in Customs and Border Protection custody – though many have parents in the US – rather than holding them for weeks in overcrowded cells, incommunicado from their desperate loved ones."

U.S District Judge Dolly Gee insisted that a "tortured interpretation" of the Flores agreement was used in attempting to indefinitely detain "blameless" migrant children whose safety "should be paramount" (Macias). Still, the practice illegally continues. Since these children have often, to public horror, been kept in massive cages, the tributes' confinement in the monkey cage seems a distinct parallel. They share a faucet, but receive no food, clothes, or medical care for five days. Rats and a rabid raccoon bite them. Afterwards, everyone blames Jessop for bringing rabies from the city. His mentor insists otherwise on camera. It's their prejudice that casts him as diseased, when their own Capitol is the source of the plague.

Capitol citizens (representing spoiled Americans, as they were in the trilogy) seem painfully out of touch. Grandma'am always thinks the worst of district children as she goes around in house slippers, pretending to live in the past. "They're not like me. They're district. That's why they belong in a cage," says a little girl. Presumably, television coverage and her family have taught her to see the other children this way. Arachne says she's visited District 10 and can craft convincing fiction about its tribute, who won't speak to her. "It's practically my second home," she claims, sounding like a tourist who's never bothered actually connecting with locals.

Coriolanus shares this attitude: When he hears that people from District 2 sprinkle breadcrumbs on the dead, Coriolanus thinks, "If you ever needed proof of the districts' backwardness, there you had it. Primitive people with their primitive customs" (224). Moreover, Coriolanus believes that he shouldn't be treated like district children. As he thinks, "It was like the Hunger Games. Only they weren't district kids. The Capitol was supposed to protect them…Certainly the child of a Snow should be a top priority" (116). All his training and education, along with his family, have taught him he is superior because he's from the Capitol.

"A world in which the Capitol citizens see their lives as perfectly normal breeds a sense of superiority that leads them to view people from poorer districts as *ab*normal, even subhuman, and in need of fixing. Their perception of their lifestyle as the norm also blinds them to the actual workings of the power systems that make it possible" (Van Dyke 259). When Coriolanus is impressed by Lucy, he casts her, publicly and within his imagination as a Capitol resident, too cultured to belong to the districts. This is a typical type of prejudice, denigrating an entire group except for one or two of its members. As Coriolanus explains to the public:

> The Covey had a long history as musical performers, were artists of a kind rarely seen, and were no more like district residents than people from the Capitol were. In fact, if you thought about it, they almost *were* Capitol, and only be a series of misfortunes had somehow landed, or quite possibly been mistakenly detained, in District 12. Surely people could see how at home Lucy Gray seemed in the Capitol? (198)

This sort of exceptionalism, hating a social group but considering one of its members a paragon who doesn't deserve the same cruelty, remains a dismissive and destructive form of prejudice. The dean accurately points out it's not breeding "but more food, nicer clothing, and better dental care" (199). This is also true of the migrants who are people like any others – just with fewer advantages, especially in detention. Coriolanus and Lucy Gray realize this strategy is working as she sings for the Capitol folks to try to establish herself as a person in their eyes. Still, Coriolanus cannot see them as his equals.

Those in the Capitol treat district kids as subhuman. After the District 10 girl kills Arachne and dies, her body is paraded about on a hook with the starving, bound filthy children below her. Such tactics have used in slave revolts through history to discourage others. They are intended as a deterrent, a punishment so horrible that no one will attempt this again. It's particularly used by the powerful to teach the powerless not to rebel – especially when the powerless are desperate enough to try. This too is the case of the migrants:

> At a briefing, officials said the threat of detention would send a message that bringing children into the United States doesn't guarantee their release. Would it? Separating families had no effect. The dangers families face on these perilous journeys have had no effect. The anti-immigrant rhetoric from the Trump administration has had no effect. There is also the matter of rights. There's no need to punish families for exercising their legal right to claim asylum at the border. They can be released on bond or with court-ordered supervision while they await hearings. ("A New Cruelty")

Many Americans were horrified by the emerging human rights violation. Much more disturbing were the number of Americans who had no problem with this. "It's their fault for coming," was the repeated refrain, despite the fact that the families were following the proper channels to seek asylum. This too has a parallel in Collins' book, as Sejanus stresses that the tributes were innocent children during the war and certainly never chose it. Neither did many of their parents, who are rural farmers and miners, not prisoners of war. Of course, the American system is perpetuating the same immoral answer as Panem's: "detention still punishes children for their parents' actions, which in many cases are not illegal." As the article's author adds, "Children and adolescents by nature are not emotionally mature. That's one reason they're blameless in accompanying their parents here. It's also why extended detention is especially traumatic for them" ("A New Cruelty"). Of course, the children are used to represent their districts, much as they committed no crime themselves.

On reaching the deprivation of District 12, Coriolanus is revolted. However, he doesn't share his food with starving children or encourage his Capitol friends to start a charity project. Instead, he judges them. "These people had given up, and some part of him blamed them for their plight." He tells his friends, "We pour so much money into the districts" that everyone in the Capitol resents them. Sejanus replies that the money goes to industry but not to the desperate families. Still, Coriolanus considers himself superior. People from the districts, as he's been raised to see them, are "Human, but bestial. Smart, perhaps, but not evolved. Part of a shapeless mass of unfortunate barbaric creatures that hovered on the periphery of his consciousness" (194).

The casually racist Capitol dwellers are embodied in Coriolanus's grandmother, who's appalled at inviting the neighbors, formerly from District Two, into her house. Likewise, she tells Coriolanus not to eat with Lucy, as it suggests equality. Grandma'am is the racist, out-of-touch old guard. She sings the anthem each morning in true thoughtless patriotism, without recalling the government's duty to provide food and safety for her family. Their entire life is about maintaining appearances, though secretly she hoards lima beans to keep them alive. This last suggests she knows deep down that the government isn't doing its job. Too many in America share this double consciousness, insisting that the government is perfect in all things as long as it stops illegal immigration. The knowledge that businesses are failing from trade wars and that climate change is causing hurricanes and heat waves is ignored. In fact, his grandmother echoes this blindered perception with a determined look toward the future. "When Coriolanus is president," his grandmother insists constantly, "everything from the rickety Capitol air force to the exorbitant price of pork chops would be magically corrected" (8). How many Americans say the same thing about getting rid of immigrants?

When Lucy saves Coriolanus's life, Grandma'am decides,

in another example of exceptionalism, "Well, like as not she decided the Peacekeepers would gun her down if she ran, but still, it shows some character. Perhaps, as she claims, she is not really district" (143). She can only accept that a district girl would save a life out of self-interest and finally praises her as being one of the Capitol people instead of "one of them." Clearly, her prejudice is blinding her completely. It's awful that people can only respect those seen as "us" rather than "them," and only deign to consider them human by admitting a few special outsiders into the circle. Scholastic editor David Levithan explains, "Not many of us manage to write books that effectively challenge readers to question how they see the world and how they see their role within it. But that's exactly what Suzanne does" (Appell). One hopes that reading this novel may provoke a little more compassion.

BACKSTORY REVEALED

- As a prequel, the story is filled with near-constant shoutouts and setup to the trilogy, as well as slightly expanded worldbuilding:
- Reaping Day is July 4.
- Tigris is Coriolanus's cousin. Tigris's talent with fashion, even in the midst of poverty, foreshadows the stylistic extravagance that the Capitol will embrace in times of prosperity, as well as her own future look.
- Grandma'am has a roof garden and pins a red rose on Coriolanus, which stabs him (a foreshadowing of the future and the final rose he will wear). She has always intended him to be president and insists he always comport himself with old-fashioned manners.
- Avoxes are enslaved by the Capitol in both times as a punishment.
- When Coriolanus is a student, the people can't afford to throw things away, and wasting food at school is punished. By Katniss's time, the Capitol citizens have turned food waste into a cultural statement as they serve purgatives at the banquet of *Catching Fire*. This may be seen as a reaction to the dimly remembered time of poverty or a way to define themselves in their own minds as rich. Coriolanus may even be employing lessons he learned in his own hungry time.
- They watch the games in Heavensbee Hall, a nod to Plutarch that shows his family has likely donated lots of money.
- Plutarch Heavensbee's assistant Fulvia Cardew is presumably a relative of Livia Cardew.

- Arachne Crane appears related to Seneca Crane, both from prominent families.
- Coriolanus thinks that the people are constantly reminded of the war – deliberately, thanks to the rubble and ration coupons. The Hunger Games just have people fighting in the same crumbling arena, without much variation or worldbuilding. Collins adds: "Even as the victor in the war, the Capitol wouldn't have had the time or resources for anything elaborate. They had to rebuild their city and the industries in the districts, so the arena really is an old sports arena. They just threw in the kids and the weapons and turned on the cameras. The 10th Hunger Games is where it all blows wide open, both figuratively and literally" ("Scholastic Releases").
- Coal miners' quotas are mentioned in chapter one.
- This is the first year with Capitol-chosen mentors. Coriolanus thinks in chapter one that mentors may prep candidates for the interviews but should also do something to excite everyone and encourage people to watch. They are students but several are killed, so the concept is to be discontinued. Later, with more victors available, these become the mentors, though Effie and those like her somewhat bridge the two roles.
- Lucy and Jessop of District 12 come up with the first idea of a team-up, as it seems.
- A parade of Roman chariots appears, but for Arachne the dead mentor's funeral. The tributes are introduced in the parade but in chains, not triumph.
- An early version of interviews appear, with mentors talking up their frightened tributes. Lucy presents last by choice, taking the position that will later go to District 12 tributes.
- Coriolanus adds sponsor gifts of food (in drones which are reprogrammed to kill someone, presumably leading to their replacement with useless parachutes).

- Dr. Gaul adds frightening killer mutations to the game for the first time. When Haymitch competes, everything in the game is beautiful and poisonous — perhaps Gaul shaped this one.

- Lucky Flickerman — presumably Caesar's father or mentor — hosts dynamically and sets a precedent. Likewise, Coriolanus invents betting, which apparently will continue. He establishes (for his own selfish purposes) that those working with tributes can't sponsor them or bet on them, a rule that continues. Sejanus says, "I heard some of the faculty talking about what a mistake it'd been to involve the students, so I think that was a one-off. But I wouldn't be surprised if we see Lucky Flickerman back again next year, or the post office open for gifts and betting" (342).

- Coriolanus's giving the silver makeup box to Lucy as a talisman later becomes policy. (Her bringing in poison that wins the game for her may set the stage for having talismans inspected.) In *Catching Fire*, Effie's gold tokens for everyone are even closer to his gift, emphasizing that they're a team.

- The Tributes are able to hide in the tunnels under the arena for the first time. This leads to a more complex show and presumably inspires tracking chips and more cameras in future.

- Lepidus jokes that they should list the survivors on the scoreboard and Snow says it's a good idea. By Katniss's time, there is indeed a sort of scoreboard with portraits in the sky.

- Turning a student into a snake-human hybrid after she's bitten (with unclear long-term effects) seems a new kind of monstrous. In fact, similar hybrids appear in *Mockingjay*. Katniss describes an attack by creatures that are "A mix of human and lizard and who knows what else" (*Mockingjay* 311). They shriek her name in a way that suggests intelligence.

- Coriolanus is banished to District 12, where he tours all the places from Katniss's time. There are few working televisions and little interest in viewing the games. He knows this will need to change.
- Both times, the mayor has a single daughter. Mayfair is spoiled and awful while Madge Undersee gives Katniss the pin that wins her allies and finally becomes a rebellion symbol.
- Lucy Gray calls the Covey "pretty birds." With their freedom and singing, they have much bird imagery. Thus, they foreshadow Katniss. Many have noted that Maude Ivory may be Katniss's paternal grandmother.
- Coriolanus passes the bakery and gets directions there from a somewhat mean woman. It may be a family trait.
- The origin of "The Hanging Tree" is revealed with the original hanging that inspired it and Lucy Gray writing it about her life. Eventually, she's forbidden to sing it and music performances are banned.
- The Covey have an easy time getting to the meadow and lake…perhaps President Snow makes it more difficult later in retaliation.
- Dr. Kay helmed the jabberjay project. She reclaims the birds for further study and use in this book. In this story arc, Coriolanus learns to use jabberjays and packs them for return to the Capitol. He uses them again in *Catching Fire*, though Katniss had assumed they had died out.
- Coriolanus proposes not only mandatory watching and more television sets available, but motivation for the districts – a new house and substantial prize money and food for all, to encourage them to feel invested and even volunteer. The Dean pays Lucy off at Games' end, possibly inspiring this idea.
- The Dean is credited with inventing the Hunger Games in school. The reality is different: Dr. Gaul assigned students to invent the most extreme

punishment possible. His friend, Crassus Xanthos Snow, got him drunk, encouraged him to fully develop the idea, and turned it in. Dr. Gaul then launched it, with the dean as its public face.

- Snow poisons the Dean – his history as a poisoner is established in the trilogy as he is poisoned himself as a result and his mouth continuously bleeds.

- As he ends the book, Snow plots to become president and enforce more ruthless games. He decides people are "creatures who need the Capitol to survive." As he thinks, "He'd continue the Games, of course, when he ruled Panem. People would call him a tyrant, ironfisted and cruel. But at least he would ensure survival for survival's sake, giving them a chance to evolve." Also, he plans to marry someone he doesn't love, like the wealthy and connected Livia Cardew (and thus eventually produce a granddaughter). He also becomes a gamemaker and has his family fortunes rise. His views of love drive him in the trilogy:

> No matter what actually becomes of her, the only other female victor of District 12 before Katniss Everdeen, her fascination for Snow, his frustration with her freedom, and his anger at both his weakness for her and at her possible other lovers drives him to follow her and eventually to convince himself that she has tricked him, that she deserves to die. He is really eliminating her as a witness to his murder of her rival, Mayfair, but his ability to rationalize even his most appalling decisions allows him to believe he is the victim. His experience with her can certainly be seen in his cynicism as the elderly President Snow and in his treatment of Katniss Everdeen, whose romance with Peeta he finds unbelievable. Surely seeing the footage of her kissing Gale only confirms his suspicions about humanity in general and women in particular, and his perverse attempts to twist Peeta into a weapon to kill Katniss are a direct result of the conclusions about love that he makes by the end of *The Ballad of Songbirds and Snakes*. (Hardy, "Ten Things")

Katniss parallels

There are many parallels between young Coriolanus and Katniss in particular, casting them as foils as well as nodding to the trilogy:

- At the beginning, Coriolanus dresses in his father's shirt as Katniss does her mother's dress. Both of these suggest costuming uncomfortably as their parents and being burdened with their ill-fitting legacies.
- His shirt has tesserae buttons. These are actually mosaic tiles, linking him with the glories of Rome, but it also recalls the "tesserae grain" Katniss earns.
- Tigris dyes Coriolanus's shirt with marigolds. Flowers are the central symbol of the district children, especially 11 and 12.
- Coriolanus must wear a tie to dinner each night, always have a clean handkerchief, maintain standards. They eat the cabbage soup off fine china. Katniss lacks most of this, but insists on keeping herself and her sister looking very clean, as she fears that if others perceive their desperation, they'll both be sent to an abusive children's home.
- "In the end, the people of the Capitol are highly disciplined—and by mechanisms that remain completely invisible to the vast majority of the citizens. (Van Dyke 260). By Katniss's time, this is the bribery of bread and circuses, but also societal disapproval for any rebellion as well as strict education on their own exceptionalism. These last qualities are also present for young Coriolanus.
- Coriolanus's early mentor Satyria Click cares about him but also drinks heavily and lacks self-control. With this, she seems a Haymitch figure.
- This book has the same obsession with food as the original trilogy. From the opening with distasteful cabbage soup, to the disappointing school meals, to the amazing bounty of Ma Plinth's treats, with special

meals like the turkey dinner when they were desperate. Coriolanus is scrawny from a poor diet. However, Snow's childhood deprivation doesn't make him generous but cruel.

* Katniss considers music "somewhere between hair ribbons and rainbows in terms of usefulness" (*Hunger Games* 211). Coriolanus feels much the same, and only knows the anthem.

* "Snow lands on top" is a family saying. This calls attention to his last name meaning. It also contrasts with humble Katniss whose name means a food hidden beneath the water that will help her survive—not win, simply endure.

* Grandma'am lives in fragile denial, paralleling Katniss's mother's fog. In both cases, the teens take every possible chance to become the family breadwinner as they know they're responsible for doing so. This theme also appears in the *Gregor the Overlander* books.

* Both Katniss and Coriolanus begin their stories dressing and hurrying off to Reaping Day, filled with responsibility as they reassure their delusional parents. Each starts with one best friend who knows everything about them and one sister figure (for Coriolanus, Tigris is both). Both receive the last mission they wanted. Both are watched everywhere they go and always aware of it. Both are always hungry and learn to manage it.

* As chapter one ends, "District 12 girl…she belongs to Coriolanus Snow" (21). All readers promptly think of the main trilogy with the Snow-Katniss tension and his power over her life.

* "Her relationship with Peeta, in all three books, is characterized by *mis*trust. She must, from the beginning, see Peeta as an enemy" (Rees). This comes from Katniss's own suspicious personality as well as the Capitol's pitting them against each other. The

Capitol, by contrast, assigns Coriolanus and Lucy to be allies, but his own ambition and jealousy pushes them apart.

* At the station, Coriolanus thinks that the train whistle meant his father's return, like the whistle signaling end of the day for the miners like Mr. Everdeen.

* Coriolanus likes cats. He likes to spend time with Boa Bell, while Katniss has a complicated relationship with her own Buttercup.

* Lucy calls him a rebel when they meet.

* Lucy Gray is memorable and sympathetic, but Coriolanus thinks that she's scrawny and female so she has no chance. This recalls another tribute. In fact, Lucy is the opposite of Katniss, reveling in performance. She remembers what things were like before and was a traveling player – the freest person of all. She's only in District 12 by chance. She's introduced with butterfly imagery – more ephemeral than tough Katniss -- while the snakes surrounding her tie her to nature but also subtly suggest duplicity and the temptation of Eden. Katniss, by contrast, is painfully forthright and doesn't know how to entertain.

* Like Katniss, Lucy Gray has dresses from the old days that let her dress better than the other kids in their gray. Both inherit them from their mothers. Jessup and Lucy hold hands on the platform. She sings with the crowd, offering a chorus of "Nothing you can take from me was ever worth keeping." This is a significant theme in the trilogy as Katniss loses her entire home with its district and then family and friends. Still, she remains resolute and loving even as the people rebuild.

* "How best to exploit her show-stopping entrance? How best to wrangle some success from a dress, a snake, a song?" Coriolanus thinks (30). This goal is

shared by all of Katniss's publicists, who frame her as their symbol.

🕊 Tigris says, "Tell her I am rooting for her" (187). This sounds like Cinna's line.

🕊 Lucy says she'll fight "like all-fire" (173).

🕊 Coriolanus lies in the street sick with swan flu and no one helps. Katniss has a similarly desperate moment when she's starving.

🕊 Coriolanus thinks that starvation is a weapon in their world.

🕊 Back in the war years, Coriolanus takes his childish red wagon to collect the lima beans, like Katniss does with her grain and oil rations. Eight-year-old Tigris learns to cook the beans since Grandma can't manage the stove. Katniss, too, must step up and keep the family fed.

🕊 Grandma'am says the story of a few tributes escaping during the bombing is dangerous since it's "just the kind of story that catches fire" (145).

🕊 Lucy tells Coriolanus about mockingjays.

🕊 It's possible that Gaul sets the bombs to scapegoat rebels, foreshadowing Alma Coin's similar act.

🕊 Like Katniss, Coriolanus has a scene where he thinks he's burning up in a fire, during the bombing.

🕊 Tigris enjoys raw meat, also seen when the Star Squad shelters in her shop.

🕊 Lysistrata Vickers mentors Jessup. She's perceptive and reminds Coriolanus they're being used. This message of mentors being as trapped as tributes returns over and over.

🕊 Like Katniss, Coriolanus himself is flung into the games. Coriolanus realizes when he's thrown into the games, "He was just like the subject of [Dr. Gaul's] other experiments, students or tributes, or no more consequence than the Avoxes in the cages" (229). Sejanus finds how to sneak in, whereas in *Catching Fire*, the team discover how to sneak out.

- Jessup and Lucy (a loyal team of the muscle and the smart one) echo Thresh and Rue. When he dies, Lucy cleans up his body like Katniss does Rue's.
- Toward the end of the games, the mentors eat lamb stew together. Cookies frosted with pretty flowers and apples appear as well, offering more food salutes. The dean needles Coriolanus at a banquet almost as treacherous as Katniss's in *Catching Fire*—at both, the teens are told they're doing a bad job deceiving others.
- In Katniss's time, the winner gets a mansion and wealth. Making Coriolanus a closer parallel, he's offered a scholarship that will likewise secure his future and his family's.
- Coriolanus advises Lucy to run from the weapon pile and hide, much as Haymitch advises Katniss. Lucy poisons two tributes, while Katniss considers doing so with nightlock berries.
- Katniss and Coriolanus (and Haymitch) all win the games by defying the rules the gamemakers have set out. All are brutally punished for their triumphs.
- Lucy calls Coriolanus "a rare bird" (123).
- Grandma'am tells him that they can't take away his being a Snow. This echoes Lucy's first song and Peeta's words to Katniss on the roof. In fact, Tigris and Coriolanus say goodbye on their roof for privacy, and Tigris takes advantage of it to criticize the system.
- Katniss promises her sister she'll be back—like Snow doing the reverse journey to District 12.
- When Coriolanus gets to District 12, he's creeped out by the forest. He also trades and listens to music at the Hob. The Covey live in the Seam and take him to see the meadow and the lake. There, the Covey fish and dig up katniss roots.
- Coriolanus is disgusted by the mockingjays. Over and over, he views them as nature "running amok" and needing to be tamed. He soon accepts the jabberjays,

which are controllable with the press of a button. There are particularly suggestive moments, when he tries to shoot the mockingjays and catch them in baited traps, but the birds evade him both times.

- Sejanus wants to be a medic, as Prim will later.
- Lucy tells Coriolanus that he found her though "the odds didn't seem in my favor" (384).
- Lucy Gray has a goat, like Prim's.
- Towards the end, Coriolanus thinks. "Nothing since the reaping had seemed very real." Peeta has similar thoughts in *Catching Fire*. Coriolanus also thinks, "Sejanus was playing with fire."
- Coriolanus and Katniss are both reluctant to bring children into such a dangerous world to suffer.
- Gale decides, "Katniss will pick whoever she thinks she can't survive without" (*Mockingjay* 329). Coriolanus makes a similar choice – his answer is Dr. Gaul. Katniss begins her relationships through artifice and survival then grows to attraction and love. Snow goes the opposite way.
- *Mockingjay* reveals that the rebels are as immoral as the tyrants, forcing Katniss to reevaluate her side and dramatically turn against it. Coriolanus comes to a similar conclusion, though with a bit less justification – he decides Sejanus and Lucy are evil killers who will bring down his society and betrays them in turn.
- *1984,* an inspiration for *The Hunger Games* with its constant surveillance, continues its parallel imagery in this book. Coriolanus, like Katniss, must watch his words, actions, and appearance lest his true situation be revealed. Further, the protagonist of *1984* knows that whatever he does in an unjust society, betraying his one true love is the one line he won't cross to maintain his humanity. Snow believes similarly of himself but finally, deliberately crosses this line.
- As he ends the book, Snow's thoughts turn to Lucy: "She could fly around District 12 all she liked, but she

and her mockingjays could never harm him again"
(516). When Katniss, a theatrical girl on fire who
sings and wear a mockingjay pin, arrives and wins her
games, she must seem like Lucy Gray returned for
vengeance.

NAMES HAVE DEEPER MEANINGS

"In her inner monologue, Katniss sees herself as the always-capable provider of food, the one who protects her family from starvation: Prim's goat, her illegal hunting, the grooslings she brings down and gives to Rue and Peeta: all are a sign that she is the feeder of others, always in control" (Frankel, *Many Faces*). Her name of katniss roots is pointedly appropriate. Joining her is Peeta (pita), "the boy with the bread"; Gale, who's like a savage windstorm; Rue—the herb of death wreathes and sorrow; and Primrose, a smoothing, youthful flower with medical applications. Opposing them are the Roman names of the Capitol, which are just as carefully chosen. Coriolanus Snow is named for the cruel hero of the Shakespeare play, who believes in feeding the Roman citizens and letting those from the provinces starve. He's joined by *Julius Caesar* characters (with a few from *Antony and Cleopatra*) who help retell the story of endless revolutions that change nothing. The names in this book frame a different story but are just as carefully chosen.

The Covey

Within Lucy Gray Baird's "Covey" (a flock of birds), as is mentioned in the book, all are named for a ballad and a color (several double as jewel colors, suggesting preciousness). These ballads are English and Scottish, nodding to the old world of books and traveling players (several are Child ballads) as well as the Celtic culture that contrasts with the Roman one. They also tie in well to the tragic structure of the novel:

> The popular, or folk, ballad is the oldest type, and it usually revolves around stock characters, like Fair Margaret, the False

> Knight in the Road, and the House Carpenter. Its themes are
> generally love and death, and it is usually serious, although there
> are a few humorous ballads, like "The Farmer's Curs'd Wife."
> These ancient songs often have a range of variant versions.
> "Barbry Allen," whose protagonist gives her name to a member
> of the Covey, probably holds the record, clocking in at around
> 158 documented versions. (Hardy, "Ballad")

Lucy Gray is named for the Wordsworth poem, as described. Her last name, Baird, suggests her bardic profession. "Lucy Gray" indeed sees the girl die and haunt the forest like a ghost, merged with nature and filled with its energy. The ballad too ends with a touching mystery:

> Yet some maintain that to this day
> She is a living Child,
> That you may see sweet Lucy Gray
> Upon the lonesome Wild.
>
> Over rough and smooth she trips along,
> And never looks behind;
> And sings a solitary song
> That whistles in the wind.

This echoes Snow's final thoughts of her: "Lucy Gray's fate was a mystery then, just like the little girl who shared her name in that maddening song. Was she alive, dead, a ghost who haunted the wilderness? Perhaps no one would ever really know. No matter—snow had been the ruination of them both. Poor Lucy Gray. Poor ghost girl singing away with her birds" (515-516). The original imagery is particularly on target, with lines about how "Her feet disperse the powdery snow, / That rises up like smoke."

Lucy Gray takes the second name from winter – a parallel to Snow, emphasizing their connection. It's also a depressing time of oppression and starvation she must fight to survive, echoing names like Gale and Everdeen (Evergreen). It must also be noted that in her desire for freedom, she pursues "gray" morality – she kills three people in the Hunger Games, but all these actions are justified not only through self-defense but because two of her victims are close to death. Her ending is also ambiguous – did she betray Coriolanus or not? Guessing is left to the reader.

Barb Azure is named for "Barbara Allen" and the serene color of the sky. In the ballad, a rich young man pleads for her love on his deathbed. However, she haughtily refuses, pointing out how he has slighted her. He dies, and finally she dies of grief. A thorn grows on his grave and a rose on hers, linking them forever.

Maude Ivory is named for "Maude Clare" and the ivory of a piano. This is the color of white but a little off for imperfect innocence as the district's troubles spill over to her. Likewise, this parallels Snow's old, cream-colored shirt at the beginning — she's the voice of innocence within that he loses in the Games. "Maude Clare" by Christina Rossetti features a beautiful young woman watching as her ex weds a less-fair bride. She pointedly returns all his gifts and their memories, dumping him in a delightfully assertive voice. While Maude Ivory is too young for romance, her independence makes this an excellent namesake poem. It also suggests Lucy Gray's relationship with Billy Taupe.

Tam Amber is named for "Tam Lin" (Child Ballad 39), a very famous ballad of the queen of the fairies abducting a young man. Janet, an assertive landowner pregnant with his child, wrestles him away from the queen of the fairies. While not much of Tam's personality is seen, he's named for this very feminist tale. His foundling aspect is also suggested as he's a baby "stolen by the fairies." Amber is a sunny color, though it's actually made from tree sap, linking him with the forest.

Clerk Carmine: Carmine or cochineal is a deep red pigment for brightness and theatricality. "Clerk Colvill" is Child ballad 42. In it, the hero ignores the advice of his lady and finds a mermaid, who seduces him. The mermaid curses him for his infidelity, and he dies. Like "Tam Lin," this story poises the hero between fairy and mortal women and worlds. The Covey, likewise, are not really Capitol or district but instead endlessly stuck in limbo.

As for Billy Taupe, Taupe is grey-brown, a color of

murkiness, even dirtiness in contrast with Maude Ivory's innocence. There are many ballad possibilities. "Billy in the Darbies" by Herman Melville, an American, doesn't fit well with the others, but neither does Billy Taupe. In it, the main character wonders about people's inherent cruelty and willfulness rather than the wide-held belief at the time that people were naturally angelic. As such, these themes tie heavily into Collins' novel. "The Ballad of Billy the Kid" by Billy Joel likewise doesn't fit the origins of the other poems, but since it's about an outlaw, it might be an inspiration too.

The female goat named Seamus is surprising in itself. Of course, one must predict that she follows the naming pattern of the humans in the family. *The Ballad Poetry of Ireland* has one, "The Boatman of Kinsale" by Thomas Davis, with a chorus of "Righ Seamus, Righ Seamus, go bragh." As the lyrics add:

> The wind that round the Fastnet sweeps
> Is not a whit more pure
> The goat that down Cnoc Sheehy leaps
> Has not a foot more sure.

This, like the others, is a love song, but this love remains faithful (perhaps suggesting that goats don't betray people).

Many ballads feature faithlessness and betrayal in love, but it must be noted that basically everyone's ballad except Lucy Gray's is this sort. Likewise, many feature love triangles between people from two worlds in particular. Lucy's has a different image, of the wandering ghost, but her being surrounded by these stories symbolizes both her past with Billy and future with Coriolanus.

The Capitol

Certainly, everyone in the Capitol has Roman names, as the Capitol echoes Rome with the districts its abused rural countryside. The original trilogy further took most of its names from Shakespeare's Roman plays, as I explore in the book *Katniss the Cattail*. This set of characters is taken from the life of Emperor Tiberius (symbolized by Coriolanus Snow) and the men and women closest to him, though less directly than the Caesar references in the trilogy. Of course, the names were not chosen randomly, but to make deliberate allusions:

Crassus Xanthos Snow is Coriolanus's distant father. In fact, Marcus Licinius Crassus helped found the Roman Empire. His power came from crushing Spartacus's slave rebellion, thus paralleling him logically with the man who defeated the Districts. He was also in a famous foundational Roman alliance, the first Triumvirate, which eventually fell apart, like the Dean's all-important friendship with Crassus Snow. He's famous for his wealth, as Snow's was, though in this case, his reputation doesn't match the reality. Xanthus was the god of the River Troy, under siege by many invading tribes, much like the Capitol itself. There were several others of that name in Greek myth, mostly famous for their epic deaths. This too is this man's main effect on the novel.

Fabricia Whatnot, "a woman as ridiculous as her name" is Tigris's boss in fashion, so her name clearly refences fabric. A whatnot can refer to a number of sewing implements as well as the cabinet that keeps them.

Remus Dolittle is the neighbor and future gamemaker whose father got him the post. His surname seems to reflect his uselessness more than the famous fictional veterinarian. His first name is from one of the mythic founders of Rome — but the one who was killed by his tougher brother Romulus. His future in the games doesn't bode well.

Pontius and Venus, gawking kids, are won over by Lucy. Venus was the goddess of beauty, most often admired rather than looking at others. Pontius Pilate was a governor of the Roman province of Judaea, under Emperor Tiberius, so the timing fits. He's most famed for condemning Jesus to execution, but this one is fortunately kinder. Both distant authoritative names here emphasize the gulf between the tributes and the Capitol dwellers.

Pluribus Bell, seller of black-market goods, has a name

that means "many." It could refer to his many products or the many personalities and costumes he brings to his shows. The surname suggests music. Further, Pluribus has the cat Boa Bell. Cats enjoy playing with both of these, suggesting playfulness and theatricality. This cat of course also nods to Buttercup and to Snow's dislike of birds.

Lucretius "Lucky" Flickerman is clearly the father or other relative of host Caesar Flickermen. A "Flickerman" is a dramatic documentary about someone's life, echoing this job interviewing the contestants. His nickname is echoed in several mentors' names which all mean happy or fortunate. Clearly, they're privileged to live in the Capitol even at such times. Titus Lucretius Carus was a Roman poet and philosopher. Lucretius's scientific poem "On the Nature of Things" inspired many future works like *The Aeneid*. Likewise, Flickerman's broadcast shapes the future games.

Lepidus Malmsey is the reporter reporting on the tributes. Marcus Aemilius Lepidus formed the Second Triumvirate alongside Octavian and Mark Antony. This required being a rather silent partner between the two stronger personalities as well as switching sides in the complex political arena. The reporter has similar challenges.

Teachers

Dr Voluminia Gaul, head gamemaker, is named for the mother of Caius Martius Coriolanus in Shakespeare's play. This figure urges her son to become more violent, and he's easily swayed. She encourages him to succeed in the military and then to take political office. When he's exiled from Rome, she channels his aggression onto the path she desires. Likewise, Dr, Gaul quickly becomes Coriolanus Snow's chief mentor and manipulates his life. Her last name is the Roman-era name for France – the equivalent of the Districts. Perhaps she's more of an outsider than she reveals.

Dean Casca Highbottom created the Games. In history, Publius Servilius Casca Longus was one of Caesar's assassins and a main character in Shakespeare's play —most characters of which starred in the original trilogy. This Casca too is devoted to bringing down the Snow family.

History professor Crispus Demigloss apparently glosses over their people's failures. Flavius Julius Crispus was a leader in victorious military operations against Gaul and Germania, and then went on to become Caesar. Since his namesake joined history by conquering the equivalent of the Districts, the more modern character is indeed likely to "gloss" over District accomplishments and tell a one-sided story.

The less-seen teachers also have significant names. Satyria Click is Coriolanus's mentor in chapter one. Her first name evokes a satyr, wise figures that nonetheless often weren't that powerful in myth. The surname may be another film reference or a nod to being in a clique — students are part of the group or not. Hippocrata Lunt is school counselor. Since Hippocrates is the father of medicine, this makes sense. The gymnasium mistress is Agrippina Sickle. Agrippina the Elder historically wedded Emperor Tiberius's heir to unite the families. She was mother to Caligula, suggesting that this gym mistress has raised selfish and violent Capitol children or even conditioned them to be so. A sickle is like Death's scythe, an ominous image though also one from agriculture.

Tributes and Mentors

In the original trilogy, Katniss doesn't learn most tributes' last names and sometimes not even the first ones. All this emphasizes the tributes' pathetic fates, not even to be recorded or remembered. This time, exacerbating this angle, nearly half die before the games begin, and then the record of the games is buried as well. Here the emphasis is even more on the mentors, who are introduced on their own list mentoring only "boy" or girl." Later, the tributes' names are added but only Lucy and Jessop have last names revealed anywhere. This lack dehumanizes and deprivileges them.

District 1: Mentors and Tributes

Livia Cardew mentors Facet. He's shot trying to escape during the bombing. His name, like Glimmer from book one, suggests part of a jewel, but in fact he's merely a facet, or small side of the Capitol's plan. Livia was an empress of Rome, wife of Caesar Augustus, who chose her not from love but to be a politically worthy wife. Coriolanus chooses this Livia, whose family are elite bankers, for similar reasons.

Palmyra Monty mentors Velvereen, whose name suggests a costly fabric that's still a commodity. She's shot trying to escape during the bombing. Palmyra, meanwhile, is an ancient Syrian city. As a silk road stop that blended Roman and Persian architecture, she appears a bridge between old and new.

District 2: Mentors and Tributes

Sejanus Plinth is from District 2, so many pick on him. His father is Strabo, a social climber willing to pull strings. A plinth is a pedestal for a statue — social climbing has been their family's total ambition. Strabo, meanwhile, was a wealthy philosopher. Just as the Roman Empire was beginning, he allied with them and was granted Roman citizenship as a reward for his contribution. The parallel seems clear.

Historically, Lucius Aelius Sejanus, from the lower part of the upper class, was the confidante and best friend of Emperor Tiberius. He gained power through the emperor, as this Sejanus does through Snow, and achieved many social reforms. Historically, he purged many people of the opposing party, while Collins' Sejanus, an idealist, never gets the chance to change the system.

Sejanus mentors Marcus, his old neighbor. He escapes during the bombing. Not much of Marcus's personality is seen, except his hatred, so it's difficult to know which Marcus, from all of history, is being referenced. For instance, this was the first name of Antony, once allied with Caesar Octavius, who then betrayed him to found his own rival empire and was killed in battle by his former friend.

Florus Friend mentors Sabyn. Sabyn evokes the Sabine women, kidnapped by the Romans. Indeed, she dies trying to escape during the bombing. Florus's name suggests he's flushed, presumably with wealth and good food. Like many mentors on this list, his name smacks of privilege.

District 3: Mentors and Tributes

Io Jasper (who's good at gene manipulation) mentors Circ (reminiscent of circuit). Io was a maiden the god Jupiter claimed, leaving his wife Juno to take a terrible revenge. The name suggests a goddess who's really a victim-princess, telling commentary on the mentors who are actually being used by those in power.

Urban Canville mentors Teslee. The name suggests a Tesla coil. Urban, of course, evokes the city. All four come from scientist families, emphasizing how much they have in common despite being on opposite sides.

District 4: Mentors and Tributes

Persephone Price mentors Mizzen, a name that references a small triangular sail. Persephone is pretty but her father Nero was a cannibal. In Greek myth, Persephone is lovely but she's the bride of Death. Further, Emperor Nero was famous for his selfishness while Rome, his capitol, was falling around him.

Festus Creed, rich from timber, mentors Coral (an ocean word, also suggesting the jewel of great price sacrificed in the Bible). His name suggests a festival, and thus his luck at being born to wealth. His last suggests belief in having fun and in the Capitol. Coral and Mizzen fight cleverly in the games as a team with Tanner (and then turn on Tanner when the moment's right) but finally each dies violently. They are products sacrificed to the Capitol.

District 5: Mentors and Tributes

Dennis Fling mentors Hy, who dies of asthma or

something similar before the games start. Hy's name, a single sad syllable, makes him seem barely there indeed. He even is part of the story only long enough for a brief hello. Dennis is derived from Dionysius, the merry wine-drinking god. Of course, the higher gods still condemned his human mother to death, in a repeated theme of sacrifice. A Fling can suggest a party, linking with other joyful mentor names.

Iphigenia Moss mentors Sol. Her father is in charge of agricultural distribution and she defiantly gives all her food away. Their dynamic introduces more parents and children at odds. Iphigenia, in Greek myth, is sacrificed by her own father to the gods so he can proceed with his ambitious plans for the Trojan War. As such, the character's expendability is stressed. Moss links with agriculture and subtly suggests she's from the districts. Sol means sun, but also suggests that this tribute is solo, alone. In fact, Iphigenia isn't even sure whether her name is Sol or Sal, giving her sacrifice even more pointlessness.

District 6: Mentors and Tributes
Apollo Ring mentors Otto, meaning wealth. His German name origin emphasizes that he's not from the Capitol's Roman traditions. Diana Ring mentors Ginnee. Generally short for Virginia or something else (like Ginny Weasley's Ginevra), this victim doesn't even get a full name, only childish nickname.

Apollo and Diana Ring are twins who deliberately dress alike. Their names, one Greek and one Roman, slightly vary the names of the sun and moon gods, twins themselves. All four die together in the arena bombing, emphasizing that the differences between them are an illusion. The arena is even a ring in itself – the twins are victims of the games as much as the tributes.

District 7: Mentors and Tributes
Vipsania Sickle mentors Treech, the tough, violent axe-wielder who's finally tricked and bitten by Lucy's snake.

Treech is urban slang for several types of insults. Vipsania Agrippina was the first wife of Emperor Tiberius, forced to divorce him and wed another, causing distress to both of them. Like her counterpart, she quietly followed the rules laid out from above, though they led to others' suffering. A sickle is an agricultural tool that suggests the Grim Reaper, decider of others' deaths.

Pliny Harrington (called Pup to differentiate from his naval father) mentors Lamina. Lamina mercy-kills Marcus and survives for some time on a tall pole before the Mizzaen-Coral-Tanner alliance kill her. The name references a thin layer of rock, emphasizing her toughness. Honor Harrington is a famous fictional commander. Pliny here suggests Pliny the Younger. He was a philosopher and imperial magistrate who wrote to and about the famous men of his day but allowed them to overshadow him.

District 8: Mentors and Tributes

Juno Phipps mentors Bobbin, whom Coriolanus beats to death – discovering his own savagery. Juno is described as "snooty," fitting for the competitive Roman queen goddess. A bobbin is a type of spool for thread – he's even lethal with a needle.

Hilarius Heavensbee mentors Wovey, a name suggesting weaving. She is poisoned and dies pathetically in the games after barely hanging together. Hiliarius presumably has an upbeat disposition (though such a name also suggests the happy circumstance of being born to wealth) and is related to Plutarch. The last name is derived from a Plutarch quote, in fact.

District 9: Mentors and Tributes

Gaius Breen mentors Panlo. This Spanish-language name adds a little diversity and may evoke the plight of the children in cages. Both tributes are injured in the bombing and die, forbidden the hospital. Meanwhile, Gaius, who loses his legs in the bombing and finally succumbs to his injuries, shares his name with Gaius Julius Caesar, who was stabbed in the back by senators he trusted. This Gaius may or may not have been killed by his teachers, but either way, as with Caesar, they use his death to encourage violence for their own aims. Further, Gaius is Coriolanus' first name in history and Shakespeare. The death and exploitation of his fellow student much like himself reminds Coriolanus Snow that he could be thrown away as easily.

Androcles Anderson mentors Sheef. This name suggests a bundle of grain, also known for being consumed. Androcles too is hospitalized after the bombing. The famous story "Androcles and the Lion" is told of a slave from Tiberius's time. He removes a thorn from a lion's paw and the lion is grateful. However, the modern Androcles fails to learn this lesson. He doesn't protect his injured tribute, who dies instead. He wants to be a reporter like his mother, but presumably will continue the tradition of Capitol callousness.

District 10: Mentors and Tributes

Domitia Whimsiwick, a dairy heiress, mentors Tanner. Many women of the *gens* Domitia from Rome were wives or relatives of the emperors. Meanwhile, Tannery is the art of converting animal skins to leather. Tanner is indeed fearsome and violent, until his own teammates betray and kill him.

Arachne Crane (whose parents build luxury hotels that seem especially callous in the face of district suffering) mentors Brandy. The child is named as a commodity, and Arachne treats her as one, mocking her with food until Brandy (a volatile substance that makes people lose their reason) kills her. In myth, Arachne's arrogance turns her into a venomous spider, so there are clear character parallels. She's likely related to Seneca Crane…both of whom enthusiastically give their souls to the gamemakers and are sacrificed by them.

District 11: Mentors and Tributes

Clemensia Dovecote (the energy secretary's daughter) mentors Reaper. As mentioned in the book, this is a grim choice of name, but the tribute was born before the reaping and thus it references a farm implement. The Grim Reaper, who takes his scythe imagery from the farmers who dreamed him up, is an inescapable mental image here. Reaper is indeed the final death and, with rabies and poison, he seems in a state of living death for quite some time. Eventually, Lucy Gray must kill him with poison and exhaustion. Though he appears the toughest, he comforts Dill who's dying of tuberculosis and shows compassion in the game. As he lines up the bodies and covers them in the flag, Clemmie stubbornly refuses to show the "clemency" of her name and send him food or water because he's not killing. "My Tribute's mentally unbalanced," she complains, while refusing to examine her own recent damage.

Clemmie's teacher Dr. Gaul has the snakes bite her for lying about writing their group project. There's neurological damage afterwards as well as a terror of snakes. Titus Flavius Clemens was great-nephew of the Roman Emperor Vespasian, executed for following his beliefs instead of the law. He was made a saint, creepily foreshadowing Clemmie's near-fate.

Felix Ravenstill mentors Dill (a humble food plant with a strong flavor like rue). He dies pathetically of tuberculosis, a victim of poverty-struck district conditions. Felix is the grandnephew of the president, with another name that means happy. Ravens, meanwhile, are ominous birds known for heralding death. This president, it seems, shares many of Snow's characteristics.

District 12: Mentors and Tributes

Lysistrata Vickers mentors Jessup Diggs. His name sounds very rural indeed, with a reference to mining and digging. Meanwhile, Lysistrata's parents are in the press, which may explain her commitment to truth. Reversing her parents' personalities as many of the mentors do, she doesn't like drawing attention to herself. Further, she's perceptive and reminds Coriolanus they're being used. She gets her name from an ancient Greek comedy in which women change the system by refusing sex until their demands are met. Thus, she has the name of a revolutionary, if a comic one.

Coriolanus Snow mentors Lucy Gray Baird. The legendary Roman leader is most famous because of Shakespeare's play, *Coriolanus*. The play opens with rioting because Gaius Marcius Coriolanus is withholding grain from the starving farmers because they're not in the military. There's a clear parallel in the characters. Coriolanus flies into a rage and gives a mighty speech of how the patricians (aristocrats) should rule over the lower classes in every way. Allowing the farmers into the senate at all is allowing "the crows to peck the eagles" (III.i.172). He's banished, but returns more powerful, with Rome at his mercy.

> Shakespeare makes Coriolanus a completely contemptible figure, so selfish and vile that he'll kill his own citizens rather than let them have a vote. At the same time, Shakespeare doesn't encourage us to understand the character, who only has one weak soliloquy in the entire play. He is no more the hero than Snow is—he's a thoroughly despicable figure who exists only to terrorize the citizens. Eventually, as with President Snow, the Romans execute him for his treachery. (Frankel, *Katniss)*

Snow is the enemy of food plants like katniss and rue, a creator of hunger and oppression. It emphasizes his cold calculation as well. A few puns and pieces of symbolism like his gifts of ice, which are received kindly in summer, add some nuance in this version.

As described in the book, Wordsworth's poem "Lucy Gray" (1799) describes a girl perpetually wandering the wilderness, haunting it forever as presumably she will her lost love.

WORKS CITED

Appell, Stephanie. "David Levithan: A Peek Behind the Curtain at the New *Hunger Games* Prequel." *BookPage,* May 2020 https://bookpage.com/interviews/25082-david-levithan-ya

Blasingame, James, and Suzanne Collins. "An Interview with Suzanne Collins." *Journal of Adolescent & Adult Literacy,* vol. 52, no. 8, 2009, pp. 726-727.

Borsellino, Mary. "Your Heart Is a Weapon the Size of Your Fist." *The Girl Who Was on Fire: Your Favorite Authors on Suzanne Collins' Hunger Games Trilogy,* edited by Leah Wilson. BenBella, 2011.

Collins, Suzanne. *The Ballad of Songbirds and Snakes.* Scholastic Press, 2020.

—. *Catching Fire.* Scholastic Press, 2009.

—. *The Hunger Games.* Scholastic Press, 2008.

—. *Mockingjay.* Scholastic Press, 2010.

Datta, Pradip K. "The Paradox of Greatness and the Limits of Pragmatism in Shakespeare's Coriolanus." *CLA Journal,* vol. 38, no. 1, Sept 1994, pp. 97-107. JStor.

Frankel, Valerie Estelle. Katniss the Cattail: An Unauthorized Guide to Names and Symbols in The Hunger Games. LitCrit Press, 2012.

—. *The Many Faces of Katniss Everdeen: Exploring the Heroine of the Hunger Games.* Winged Lion Press, 2013.

Granger, John. "Mockingjay Discussion 15: The Hanging Tree." *Hogwarts Professor,* 25 Aug 2010. https://www.hogwartsprofessor.com/mockingjay-discussion-15-the-hanging-tree

—. "Mockingjay Discussion 16: Katniss' Meadow Song." *Hogwarts Professor,* 26 Aug 2010.

https://www.hogwartsprofessor.com/mockingjay-discussion-16-katniss-meadow-song

Hardy, Elizabeth Baird. "The Ballad of Songbirds and Snakes, First Thoughts on a Sad, Familiar Song." *Hogwarts Professor*, 20 May 2020. https://www.hogwartsprofessor.com/the-ballad-of-songbirds-and-snakes-first-thoughts-on-a-sad-familiar-song/comment-page-1/#comment-1525262

—. "The Ballad of Songbirds and Snakes: Top Ten Pointers to the Trilogy." *Hogwarts Professor*, 4 June 2020. https://www.hogwartsprofessor.com/the-ballad-of-songbirds-and-snakes-top-ten-pointers-to-the-trilogy

—. "Guest Post: Elizabeth Hardy Takes A Bird's Eye View: Birds in Suzanne Collins's *Hunger Games*." *Hogwarts Professor*, 22 Mar 2010. https://www.hogwartsprofessor.com/guest-post-elizabeth-hardy-takes-a-bird%e2%80%99s-eye-view-birds-in-suzanne-collins%e2%80%99s-hunger-games

Hatlen, Burton. "The 'Noble Thing' and the 'Boy of Tears': Coriolanus and the Embarrassments of Identity." *English Literary Renaissance,* vol. 27, no. 3, Fall 1997, pp. 393-420. JStor.

Hobbes, Thomas. *Leviathan,* edited by Edward White and David Widger. 1651. Project Gutenberg, 2009.

Levithan, David. "The Hunger Games: An Exclusive Look from Page to Screen." New York Comic-Con, 10 Oct 2020. https://www.youtube.com/watch?v=O1WF2LUUFBg

Locke, John. *Two Treatises of Government,* edited by Thomas Hollis. 1764. A. Millar et al., 2019.

Long, Clara. "Written Testimony: "Kids in Cages: Inhumane Treatment at the Border": Testimony of Clara Long Before the U.S. House Committee on Oversight and Reform, Subcommittee on Civil Rights and Civil Liberties," *Human Rights Watch,* 11 July 2019. https://www.hrw.org/news/2019/07/11/written-testimony-kids-cages-inhumane-treatment-border

Macias Jr, Martin. "White House Bid to Indefinitely Detain Migrant Child." *Courthouse News,* 10 July 2018 https://www.courthousenews.com/judge-strikes-down-white-house-bid-to-indefinitely-detain-migrant-child

Neumeyer, Peter F. "Ingratitude Is Monstrous: An Approach to Coriolanus." *College English,* vol. 26, no. 3, Dec. 1964, pp. 192-198. JStor.

"A New Cruelty, Detaining Families Indefinitely." *Express-News Editorial Board,* 26 Aug 2019. https://www.expressnews.com/opinion/editorials/article/A-new-cruelty-detaining-families-indefinitely-14379954.php

"News Room," *Scholastic.com,* 17 June 2019. http://mediaroom.scholastic.com/press-release/scholastic-publish-new-novel-worldwide-bestselling-hunger-games-series-suzanne-collins

Proser, Matthew. "Coriolanus: The Constant Warrior and the State." *College English,* Vol. 24, No. 7, Apr., 1963, pp. 507-512. *Jstor.*

Rees, Elizabeth M. "Smoke and Mirrors: Reality vs. Unreality in the Hunger Games." *The Girl Who Was on Fire: Your Favorite Authors on Suzanne Collins' Hunger Games Trilogy,* edited by Leah Wilson. BenBella, 2011.

Rousseau, Jean-Jacques. *The Social Contract and Other Later Political Writings,* edited and translated by Victor Gourevitch, Cambridge University Press, 1997.

"Scholastic Releases New Interview with Suzanne Collins, Author of the Worldwide Bestselling Hunger Games Series." *PR Newswire,* 19 May 2020.

Stipulated Settlement Agreement, Flores v. Meese, 2:85-cv-4544 (C.D. Cal. 1997).

Stone, Merlin. *When God Was a Woman.* Harcourt Brace, 1976.

Wilkinson, Lili. "Someone to Watch Over Me: Power and Surveillance in the Hunger Games." *The Girl Who Was on Fire: Your Favorite Authors on Suzanne Collins' Hunger Games Trilogy,* edited by Leah Wilson. BenBella, 2011.

Wordsworth, William. "Lucy Gray." *The Reader,* 1799.
https://www.thereader.org.uk/featured-poem-lucy-gray-
by-william-wordsworth
—. "The Tables Turned." 1798. *Poetry Foundation,* 2020.
https://www.poetryfoundation.org/poems/45557/the-
tables-turned
Van Dyke, Christina. "Discipline and the Docile Body:
Regulating Hungers in the Capitol." *The Hunger Games and
Philosophy: A Critique of Pure Treason,* edited by Nicolas
Michaud, and George A. Dunn, John Wiley & Sons,
Incorporated, 2012, pp 250-264. ProQuest Ebook Central

SONGBIRDS, SNAKES, & SACRIFICE

ABOUT THE AUTHOR

Valerie Estelle Frankel is the author of over 75 books on pop culture, including *Doctor Who – The What, Where, and How, Sherlock: Every Canon Reference You May Have Missed in BBC's Series 1-3,* and *How Game of Thrones Will End.* Many of her books focus on women's roles in fiction, from her heroine's journey guides From Girl to Goddess and Buffy and the Heroine's Journey to books like *Women in Game of Thrones* and *The Many Faces of Katniss Everdeen.* She's also written the award-winning Henry Potty parody series. Once a lecturer at San Jose State University, she's now teaching at Mission College and San Jose City College. Come explore her research at www.vefrankel.com.